# Queer Theory and Social Change

The emergence of Queer theory during the past decade represents a huge leap in our understanding of lesbian, gay, bisexual, and transgendered peoples. It has opened up new approaches for treating sexuality and gender as subjects worthy of consideration in their own right, rather than as offshoots of general cultural theory.

*Queer Theory and Social Change* argues that there is a crisis within Queer theory over whether or not its theories can actually deliver change. Max H. Kirsch argues that, even though the new social movements of the 1960s may not have succeeded in integrating diverse segments of the population, this does not foreclose the usefulness of the theories they drew on, such as political economy, for analyzing exploitation, inclusion, and our current social conditions.

*Queer Theory and Social Change* presents a challenging alternative to the current fascination with postmodern analyses of identity, culture, and difference. It emphasizes the need for a discussion of the importance of communities and the role of globalization in queer movements.

**Max H. Kirsch** is Associate Professor at Florida Atlantic University.

# Queer Theory and Social Change

Max H. Kirsch

London and New York

First published 2000
by Routledge
11 New Fetter Lane, London EC4P 4EE

Simultaneously published in the USA and Canada
by Routledge
29 West 35th Street, New York, NY 10001

*Routledge is an imprint of the Taylor & Francis Group*

Typeset in Perpetua by Taylor & Francis Books Ltd
Printed and bound in Great Britain by T. J. International Ltd, Padstow,
Cornwall

*British Library Cataloguing in Publication Data*
A catalog record for this book is available from the British Library

*Library of Congress Cataloging in Publication Data*
Kirsch, Max H., 1953–
    Queer theory and social change / Max H. Kirsch.
    Includes bibliographical references and index.
    1. Homosexuality – philosophy. 2. Lesbianism – philosophy.
    3. Social change. 4. Gay men – social conditions.
    5. Lesbians – social conditions. 6. Gay and lesbian studies.
    I. Title.
    HQ76.25 .K57 2000
    306.76'6–dc21    00-055222

ISBN 0–415–22184–6 (hbk)
ISBN 0–415–22185–4 (pbk)

# Contents

# Acknowledgements

Students and faculty at Oberlin College stimulated the inception of this work while I was in residence there during 1997–1999. This stimulation continued as I moved to direct Florida Atlantic University's new PhD Program in Comparative Studies, the Public Intellectuals Program, where the role of academia and the "state of theory" in our present social context are arenas of ongoing discussion. At Oberlin, I particularly would like to thank William Norris, who was forced to listen to early attempts at providing a grounding for this work, and contributed a careful reading at the manuscript's final stages. Too stubborn to heed all of his suggestions, I acknowledge that the resulting faults are wholly my own. The students who participated in a seminar on Queer theory helped to clarify questions of identity and social action while critically evaluating the ideas of a teacher from another generation who could not always remain in sync with their experiences. Their contribution is substantial.

At Florida Atlantic, discussions with colleagues and friends helped to interpret ideas that were in danger of becoming overly complicated and abstract. I am grateful for their willingness to listen and to help create an atmosphere where a new director of a new program could attempt to get some of his own work accomplished. Stefanie Gapinski made that atmosphere possible. Particular thanks are due to Mike Budd, who willingly and repeatedly discussed questions of class and community, and to Susan Buck Morss, who suggested that I look into the connections between class and discourse. Nawal El Saadawi read an earlier draft of the manuscript with care, offering ideas and discussion of its contents. I would also like to thank Teresa Brennan for her editing skills, and for her suggestions on a draft of this work that included the need to discuss Foucault in more detail.

For ongoing support, the time and encouragement of Patricia Cooper, Robert Gatto, Susana Meyer, and Chris and Calixte Stamp was and is, as always, invaluable. Finally, as I move along in my own career, I am constantly aware that I owe an enormous amount of gratitude to three anthropologists who saw me through my years of graduate school and the development of my own point of view. The work of June Nash, Eleanor Leacock, and Eric Wolf has been an enormous influence on me, not only because of its extraordinary concern with human rights and the systemic consequences of our current social context but also because of its commitment to a consistent reevaluation and critique of social theory. This work is an outcome of their teachings and their support. They are not responsible for its shortcomings.

# Introduction

> The sense of our own identity is fluid and tolerant, whereas our sense of the identity of others is always more fixed and often edges towards caricature. We know within ourselves that we can be twenty different persons in a single day and that the attempt to explain our personality is doomed to become a falsehood after only a few words. To every remark made about our own personal characteristics we would want, in the interest of truth, quite disregarding vanity, to say, "yes, but ...", or "that may have been true once but it is true no longer" ...
>
> (A.N. Wilson, *Incline Our Hearts*, London: Penguin, 1990)

I am an anthropologist, a gay man, a white American, a university professor. We are now accustomed to hearing individuals identify themselves and their positions in this manner, clarifying presumed prejudices, experiences, and points of view. The identification assumes a certain responsibility in reportage: if I am a gay man, can I comment on the personal violence of racial inequality, or the lesbian experience? If I am a university professor, what is it that I can say about the lives of those who work in factories? These are questions of identity, but they are also positions of credibility. They limit what we can feel comfortable asserting for those unlike ourselves, the abstraction of the "other" that has become the object of so much debate in contemporary social thought. But what we now also hear in attempts at positioning the self is the negation of description: we do not feel comfortable being labeled at all, at marking our personal experiences by applying assumptions that limit our possibilities of being or becoming. We have, therefore, also become accustomed to another kind of assertion, one that posits the limits of assuming identity at all. It is found in statements about personal composition but against labeling and identity – "I am gay, not gay; American, not American; an academic, not an academic." Those who accept the former, or "meta-identity," position argue that "I do not feel comfortable in commenting on who I am not and what I do not know." The latter, or "quasi-identity," formulation asserts independence, leading to statements of "I do not feel comfortable being told who I am. I cannot comment on the situation of others, whose experience I cannot know."

These positions stem from different projectories and histories in social theory and thought, but they can result – and have resulted – in the same consequence. Questions of credibility have created a polarization among those of us who are in objectifiably similar positions: we are all being oppressed by a larger social structure with power and the means to enforce points of strategy and view. In contesting the ability to identify with others, movements for social change have become fragmented and demoralized. The focus has shifted to the "self," the "I am the place where something has occurred," which Lévi-Strauss made famous in his *Tristes Tropiques* (1973). How has this happened?

The question is fundamental, and is central to the present work. My aim is to trace the development of these personal positions and elucidate the resulting consequences for self-actualization and social action. Meta-identity and quasi-identity statements reinforce each other, reflecting untenable attempts to achieve self-actualization. They model current social conditions and a general pessimism that has overtaken much of Western culture, at least for the moment. If, as I believe, however, it is possible to separate identity from identification, or identifying *with* from identifying *as* (or against), we can start to differentiate between individuals and individuation – the latter, I believe, being the mode of theory-building that has taken over discussion in much of postmodern and post-structuralist debate.

I approach these problems of identity, social theory, and social change from the perspective of all the self-descriptive statements I have already made, but I do not believe that these characteristics limit my ability to comment on or to empathize with the position of others. My analysis is informed by anthropology, but it is also interdisciplinary, and activist-oriented. In using anthropology as a focus for analytical statements, I note that the discipline stresses particular peoples, places, and times, comparing the variances and similarities among them. It is this aspect of anthropology's grounding of theory with observation and ethnography that allows for a more comprehensive analysis of "the social" and the individual's place in that realm. Here there is recognition that, above all else, humans are social animals, and we require communities in which to survive and to thrive.

## The reception of theory

This work is, in part, the outcome of a query into how Queer theory came to gain prominence in university halls and classrooms during the 1980s and 1990s. As an anthropologist interested in social change, Queer theory seemed to me a very tricky genre, a nexus of ideas that grew out of a myriad of social forces, successes, and failures that have enveloped left politics and theory since the 1960s. I was also fascinated by the ready and aggressive acceptance of this theory in the academy, particularly by students in the 1990s. It seemed curious how quickly elements of "queer" became accepted as received wisdom, as if students were more intent on finding ways of individuating themselves from others (and from society in general) than critically evaluating the theory being presented. To be sure, part of this acceptance can be explained by youthful energies that are focused on discovering who one is, and more often, what one is not. It is part of the "I matter most" philosophy in which individualism, subversion, and social resistance are equated. This conjoining of complex issues is encouraged by a culture that is now more than ever oriented towards separating the individual from the social, promoting an ideal that we are all unique, special, unfettered by structural forces outside our control. These positions are indeed related to the place of the individual in society as this place has evolved during the twentieth century.

Why should this generation of students find this line of thought so rewarding? It is easy to speculate that students of a traditional college age are acting normally in their desire to test the limits of their own realities. But why did academic departments, especially in the humanities, so readily staff their ranks with those professing a direction that refocuses research and teaching from critical social theory to an obsession with the individual and the subject (or lack thereof), and personal "rights"? While certainly there has been a movement in academic institutions to "please" and therefore retain students, there is a larger recounting here. For this body of theory has also been proven to have enormous appeal to an older generation of scholars, particularly those who experienced or were exposed to the social movements of the 1960s. Those who espouse the philosophy of individualism, in all its various forms, are influenced by what we know to be the limitations of movements for cultural reform and declarations of insurgency. That these movements did not succeed in fundamentally transforming Western society plays a large part in the agreement of students and professors in the call for the death of grand theory, the expulsion of what Lyotard (1984) called the "meta-narrative."[1] If there was a failure to transform the basic reproductive relations of society, what caused it? For many it was a perceived dependence on outdated Marxist renderings of capitalist social relations that excluded rather than included different points of view.

The 1960s were a time of great turbulence, with many of the participants on college campuses the same age as today's "traditionally aged" students. During this era a split emerged between the "new left" and the "old left," or those who had been involved in radical politics through the Communist Party, various socialist organizations, and of course, unions. The Free Speech movement at Berkeley, the takeover of Columbia University, the shootings at Kent State University and elsewhere were all related to a fundamental questioning of social relations as much as they were calls for the independence and autonomy from the larger social structure by the participants. Yet tremendous in-fighting characterized organizations spurred by the 1960s, where it became clear that the dominant social relations of the culture at large were also in play inside organizations. Opposing a leadership that was predominantly white and male, many women, those of color, and those with gender and sexual preferences other than heterosexual ones, felt excluded from having any real say in planning or day-to-day activities. The reactions to the organization of leadership inside the movements were supported by a global questioning of dominance by peoples struggling for their voices to be heard in the fights for national recognition and independence from colonial powers.

Within universities and colleges across the nation and over the globe, analyses of social issues began to encompass the concerns of constituencies that had also been excluded from academic theory-building. Feminist writers, in particular, changed the landscape of disciplinary directions, reinterpreting classic texts as they forged new ground concerning the place of women in society. Race, sex, and class also became central issues, building new paradigms for the inclusion of categories that had been previously secondary in analyses of social life.

These reinterpretations and other writings took place in the context of "modernist" presumptions associated with the period of the Enlightenment, the rapid social change of the seventeenth and eighteenth centuries. This historical period marked the end of the dominance of Christianity, which in its essence foretold the end of the world. Enlightenment philosophy, clearly reflected in the writings of Durkheim, Weber, and Marx, assumed a constantly changing environment that would constantly revoke the constraints of the past. The political revolutions of 1848 marked the succession of Enlightenment goals, the calls of "equality," "fraternity," and "solidarity" solidifying a notion of "rational criticism" and "progress" that is still very much with us today.

The feminist and other theory-changing paradigms that are indebted to Enlightenment philosophies have now been overtaken by charges that they, too, were not inclusive enough to represent the experience of individuals, persons, and "selves." There has been a gradual takeover of analyses of relations of resistance and alliance by the phenomenon of "discourse," which began to replace "class" as the unit of analysis of much of contemporary social theory, while the individual of bourgeois capitalism was replaced by "individual experience." But this is not a complete description of what occurred: for during the postmodern turn, at least in the United States, the focus of dissatisfaction changed from the capitalist system of reproduction to the modes of resistance of the left. This was in part due, as noted, to the perceived failure of the 1960s to meet various goals of new social movements. It was also due to the experience of many of its participants, who complained that that they were not involved, but were in fact excluded, not only from day-to-day activity but also from devising the strategy of the movements themselves. The reaction again was to demonize the "Marxist left" as a whole, as exclusionary and divisive.

The assertion of "self" has resulted in a crisis of description and of explanation that has been played out in postmodernist and post-structuralist writings. What is important to note here is that these movements, if we can use the term "movements" loosely, are not proactive. They are primarily "anti": anti-subject, anti-identity, anti-statement. This presentation fits well into a current generation's unwillingness to be labeled. These generations of ideas are thus complementary, both in the sense of age grade (again, the age of those participating in the movements of the 1960s is the same as those of today's students, and therefore, we can argue, prone to the same self-questioning), and of resistance to authority presented in the guise of theory.

The story continues. All of these developments occur in the realm of social life and social change. As we are all aware, much has changed in the world as we knew it in the 1960s and 1970s. Independence movements have enveloped world politics. Globalization has become a major player in daily social life, as much of basic production has shifted from the Euro-centered countries to the former colonial states. Multinationals and indigenous social movements have taken the world stage. At the same time that the face of re-industrialization in former colonial states mimics the look of early industrialization in the capital-intensive countries, the phenomenon of globalization has exposed the populations of the West to different forms of social organization, bringing in experiences and visions that were unnoticed during colonial rule. We can argue that it is this horizontal integration that has led many academic theorists to question our own experiences and our own visions of the world, questioning the tenets of universalism that have been in place since the 1700s. This view fits well into Clifford Geertz's (1973) assertion that one cannot have a general view of culture, but only of specific cultures. But we need to remember, as Bridget O'Laughlin reminds us, that a "vulgar" universalism is not the same as a general theory through which to interpret social representations and organization (1975: 348). Russell Jacoby (1999), among others, also decries the abandonment of universalism in the movement towards particularism, noting that cultural studies and its derivatives ultimately result in an advocacy of the status quo, enacted by those in university positions with status and renown. Jacoby argues that the "inclusiveness" of universalism implies conformity for these scholars, the real experience and oppression of the marginalized people to which those writers so often refer are lost in the drive towards the local and the unique.

We all live in social contexts through which our visions can be interpreted. We can argue that the development of new social theory that attempted to incorporate cultural difference more fully was not a denial of Marxism but a project to enrich it with a more fluid analysis of the "superstructure." But the emphasis on difference has turned out to be a slippery slope, for in the same way that theorists and activists had been assessing the "base" as objectified, the "superstructure" became the focal point. A reasoned account of political economy was made to disappear.

The use of the term "culture" in this discussion as an alternative to narrowing the subject of analysis has become enigmatic. Culture can represent anything and everything the writer has in mind. Within the academic disciplines, the usefulness of the concept of culture has raised many questions. Wolf (1982; 1999) contends that it is overused, blurring the nexus of relationships that encompass social life, while Butler (1998) wonders whether the accusation of her work as "merely cultural" devalues the concept of culture as a unifying social description. Academic Marxists have been faulted for equating culture with ideology, as a way of analyzing relationships of power (Edgar and Sedgwick, 1999: 222). Whatever the criticism, it is clear that "culture" is now contested, both by those who classically employed it to differentiate among peoples and by those who claim that the concept never really accomplished that goal.

I believe that the reports of the demise of the concept of culture have been overstated. It is still regularly applied to aspects of social life beyond labor and reproduction, and some, such as Butler, have used it to describe society as a whole. We still speak of "queer culture" and the "dominant culture" as we speak of "the culture" of others and of our own. I will offer in this volume "a working definition of culture," in an effort to situate concepts of beliefs and experience that in Western societies we share in common, and that are codified into our conceptual world without particular foresight. I will therefore talk of "the culture of novelty" and of "part-cultures" in the following pages, delineating aspects of our shared experience that directly influence our perceptions and our behavior. As I hope will become clear, it is still useful, with the caveat that it should be contextualized and identified before its use as a descriptive tool.

## Generations of understanding and practice

How do we resolve these dilemmas? While teaching an undergraduate class on Queer theory, it became quickly obvious to me that the students did not have the same questions about "queer" that I did, and that in fact the question really did not interest them. When I asked them to think about queer analytically, to define what the categories of lesbian, gay, bisexual, and transgender represent and how this assumed coalition of "LGBT" peoples operates, I was accused by a few of forcing Gay and Lesbian Studies down their throat.[2] They wanted this class to be a discussion of identity – on their own terms. These terms are not about theory, but validation. For them, the goals are a general awareness of difference, an understanding of inclusion and human rights in the broadest sense. They include anything other than the status quo. It means a differing lifestyle from what they perceive as mainstream, a different kind of cognitive supermarket where granola is next to the milk instead of cream cheese.

These students possess what Castells (1997) refers to as a "resistance identity," generated by those in devalued positions, the basis of what we commonly know as identity politics. What they do not yet possess is a "project identity" where, as Castells notes, "social actors, on the basis of whatever cultural materials are available to them, build a new identity that redefines their position in society, and, by doing so, seek the transformation of the social structure" (1997: 43). A resistance identity allows an exclusion of the excluders by the excluded, the building of identity in Foucault's terms. But "excluded" for them can range from gender to clothing style to music: they do not have a specific project in mind, but a determination to assert themselves as individuals. Perhaps this is due in part to the inherent fluidity of identity, to the reality that our versions of ourselves change regularly and for them even more often. This generational-based questioning of identity-building, along with acquiescence about the consequences of theory for social action, can be unsettling.

The use of identity for the construction of theory and action is a main project of this book. I acknowledge the problems with this concept. I hope that by the conclusion of this work, the reader will note that identity is not a stable category. There are limits, particularly within sex and gender, to which identity can be applied. Certainly research has shown that there are many men who sleep with men but do not categorize themselves as either gay or bisexual; there are many women who are lesbians for a time but initiate stable relationships with men; there are self-defined lesbians who sleep with men, or who are married. In more conservative regions, it is still common for men who are self-identified gay men to be married and with children. If we glance at the ethnographic record, the definitions become even more problematic: many cultures use male homosexuality in coming of age ceremonies; the old assumption that British boarding school boys regularly sleep with each other is true, but most of these boys do not ultimately identify themselves as homosexual. In other words, there is a limit to what temporal experience can tell us about sexuality and gender. My aim is to use identity as a mode of affiliation rather than strictly as a category of personal definition. Here identity, however short-lived, becomes essential, and dismissing its possibilities for the assertion of common goals becomes a blueprint for dismissal. Indeed, in their introduction to an anthology of lesbian cultural criticism, Susan Wolfe and Julia Penelope worry that current theory does just that. In their words:

> we cannot afford to allow privileged patriarchal discourse (of which Post-structuralism is but a new variant) to erase the collective identity lesbians have only recently begun to establish … For what has in fact resulted from the incorporation of a deconstructive discourse, in academic "feminist", discourse at least, is that the word *lesbian* has been placed in quotation marks, whether used or mentioned, and the existence of real lesbians has been denied, once again.
>
> (1993)

The key word here is collective, the alliances that are made on common grounds whether through identity *as being* or identity through cause.

I will argue in the following chapters that Queer theory, much of which deconstructs collective community, encourages political apathy as it relativizes all sexuality and gender. The fact that reclaiming queer as a name strips it of its homophobic power has validity. But the post-structuralist arguments around language that have pervaded Queer theory have diluted this reclamation as the meanings of words begin to disappear altogether. The same argument can be made for the analysis of cultural artifacts – literature, cinema, and the like – where Queer theory, arising from cultural studies, has made the most inroads. But if we redefine literature as queer rather than straight, whom are we redefining it for? When does it become absurd to deny the structural power of the dominant culture, and when does it turn to wishful thinking?

In ways that I will later explore, post-structuralism in particular is about ideas rather than action. The popularity of this methodology in Queer theory, seen most clearly in the work of Judith Butler, arrives from our students' lack of interest in defining themselves and their peers. With Butler we have a theorist, perceived as queer *and* radical, who rejects *all* categories of identity, claiming that resistance is through the refusal to identify with the other (which would thereby produce a normative subject). For her, "the prospect of *being* anything, even for pay, has always produced in me a certain anxiety, for 'to be' gay, 'to be' lesbian seems to be more than a simple injunction to become who or what I already am." She is therefore,

> not at ease with lesbian theories, gay theories, for as I've argued elsewhere, identity categories tend to be instruments of regulatory regimes, whether as normalizing categories of oppressive structures or as the rallying points for a liberatory contestation of that very oppression.
>
> (1993a: 307–308)

But I wonder, if we don't have rallying points, from where do we fight prejudice and exploitation? The notion that organizing against oppression is a "regulatory regime" is not a promising starting point for politics and collective action. Can we hope that people will come to their senses? Foucault has argued that participating in a homosexual perspective admits a homophobic discourse; yet how do we deny homophobia? We cannot simply disclaim, as Butler asks us to (1993a: 308). She would like to talk about lesbianism without referring to heterosexuality. Perhaps when these terms did not have any meaning, before the nineteenth century, this ambition might have been possible. But given the current social relations of power, it is not possible now.

Mark Lilla (1998) suggests that there has been a depoliticization of social life in academic circles that can be traced to the development of theory in France after the First World War that devalued political philosophy, understood, as he says, "as disciplined and informed reflection about a recognizable domain called politics"

(1998: 36). Furthermore, the subsequent use of language as part of a decontructionist methodology, informed by Foucault and Derrida, among others, led to the place of politics being viewed as relative and with no inherent meaning. With this genesis came the negation of all assumed categories, including gender and sexuality.[3]

Lilla also argues that the beleaguering fact of the holocaust, the failure of postcolonial experiments in Africa and Asia, the collapse of the Soviet bloc, and the aftermath of the struggles of 1968 left French radicals seriously doubting their premises (1998: 41). On the other hand,

> These same events have had no appreciable effect on American intellectual life, for the simple reason that they pose no challenge to our own selfunderstanding ... That the anti-humanism and politics of pure will latent in structuralism and deconstruction ... are philosophically and practically incompatible with liberal principles sounds like an annoying prejudice.
>
> (Lilla, 1998: 41)

The contrasts between American and European realities are most exacerbated in the protected environment of the academy, where one is free to develop methodologies of thought that have no discernible consequences. In my view, the post-structuralist stance, as most evidenced by Judith Butler, seems a rather obvious form of political naivety, but it is often not recognized as such. My students were not interested in critiques of Judith Butler, for she serves their desire to see themselves as unique. They have never experienced a social movement, and given their relative state of privilege, they may never have to assert their collectivity. For them, gender and sexuality are simply individual choices.

The gay and lesbian movements of the 1970s and 1980s politicized the conditions of everyday life and everyday culture. Almost everything we do, all art we create, all writing we do, is consciously or unconsciously political: it comes from somewhere, it supports a particular point of view. But this abstract view of politics becomes more difficult when we start to consider social change and social movements. To say that everyday life is political does not guarantee that a political program is in place.

If our goal, then, is to create a society that accepts difference, welcomes diversity, and champions human rights, how do we get there? The relativity of identity and experience is not enough. We need to confront power in all of its aspects: who holds it, how hegemony is maintained, what the dominant culture consists of and how it influences our daily lives *and* experiences. Strategies for change need to be connected and collective. This means that we need to refocus analytic energies, realizing that consciousness and action towards basic social change are interconnected; consciousness does not act on its own. There needs to be an identification process with social movements and with each other. In short, we still need to consider class, race, and history.

For my students, who are a product of the times as well as their age grade, I believe we need to pose the questions that matter. For the students of the 1960s (where the project was to form identity that differed from that of one's elders), the question posed by Terry Eagleton remains to be asked of past perceptions of political defeat:

> *what if this defeat never really happened in the first place?* What if it were less a matter of the left rising up and being forced back, than of a steady disintegration, a gradual failure of nerve, a creeping paralysis? What if the confrontation never quite took place, but people *behaved* as if it did?
>
> (Eagleton, 1997: 19)

## The organization of this work

What I have outlined above will be elaborated in the following chapters. As a whole, this work endeavors to emphasize a simple point: we are not alone, and we cannot act alone if we are to work towards social change. Examining the way in which we are *thought* to be alone, thought to be autonomous and atomized, requires both an analysis and a critique of individualism as the separated self in general *and* the positing of an alternative view that firmly locates us in the realm of the social.

This work relies and builds on those others, sometimes prominent, sometimes less visible but still productive, who work on theory and outlines of practice that concern the problems of inequality, culture, gender, and the analysis of capitalism. Necessarily, much of this work is ultimately concerned with change. We ask the following questions: What can be done to move queer movements forward? What is the role of Queer theory and its creators in movements that ultimately confront the inequality that is endemic in our society, and posit alternatives and projects for change? What is the relationship between what is now referred to as Queer theory and other kinds of theory, other social movements? The reader will note that my perspective challenges the direction that Queer theory has taken and intends to show the dangers that this direction foretells. But ultimately, the hope is to show that possibilities do exist for social change and that the fact that this discussion is taking place at all points to the possibility of a future where inequality is not assumed as a basic fact of life. To do this, we have to look closely at our past, our relationship with the theory that has been developed, and the nature of the movements that have confronted basic issues of discrimination and unequal access to resources. We need to observe what the dominant culture is telling us and to understand what it means to involve ourselves in directions that are well underway, and, furthermore, to assess the successes and failures of what has already occurred. This means not only positing the new but also delving into the underlying assumptions of theories now in vogue and providing productive critiques. We have therefore to confront our own position in society, as well as the position of others.

Chapter 1 examines our current state of politics, the environment in which we operate. It also, albeit briefly, considers the postmodern turn, and, for our present purposes, its primary theorists. The chapter situates these developments in the academic context, examining how the use of discourse came to replace class in analyses of the social, creating a new political context.

Chapter 2 considers what has become identified as Queer theory, its origins, and the contributions it has made to alleviating the condition of oppressed minorities. It reflects on the "queering of culture," the historical origins of queer thought, and the analysis of power in capitalist social formations. In considering class and the resistance it engenders, I also discuss the role of ideology in the formation of a dominant culture, including the structural schisms between the personal and the political. I provide a "working" definition of culture, noting the problems that the concept raises while proposing a version for our purposes.

Chapter 3 looks more closely at gender and the debates that have evolved surrounding it, including the constructionist/essentialist debate and the arguments about the representation of the body in society. Here the deconstruction of gender is more fully explored, along with the resultant focuses on experience and relativity. This chapter asserts that all arguments around gender exist in relation to debates over heterosexuality and the ability or inability to explore personal experiences on an individual basis.

Chapter 4 looks more closely at the description and analyses of capitalist economic formations. Class, race, sex, and gender are all categories that receive acknowledgement in the queer literature, but they are rarely fully analyzed. What does class mean in relation to Queer theory? How is it related to race, sex, and gender? Are there similarities that can be applied to our discussion, or does the reality that class cross-cuts these other categories make it less useful for analysis? My hope is that, through a careful examination of the way in which capital structures social life, creates bounded individuals, and acts to destroy communities, we can build on lessons already learned and return class to a discussion of gender, sexuality, and social movements in late capitalist society.

Chapter 5 directly addresses postmodernism and post-structuralism in the light of political economy. Queer theory has been singularly influenced by the popularity of postmodern and post-structuralist thought and the deconstructing paradigms that accompany them. The politics of post-structuralism is addressed in an effort to show that dangers exist when a school of academic thought diminishes and excludes others, in a gesture of exclusion which is at odds with their belief in inclusiveness. The excluded others include those studying class and political economy.

Chapter 6 moves the discussion from the analysis of culture to the realm of social action, placing the categories of race, sex, gender, and class firmly in the political arena, and emphasizing the need to *identify with* social movements rather than solely *identify as* an individualized "I."

The conclusion of this work reflects back on the notion of community and its role in providing a vehicle for the true subversion of oppression. It provides a discussion of strategy and of the role of civil society in this process. Finally, in light of previous discussions, it revisits the notion of "Queer" theory, proposing that we rediscover the importance of the place of community as the site where interdependence is enacted and mutual protection ensured.

# Part I

# Positioning Queer theory

# 1 Crossroads

## The current dilemma

In the summer of 1998, Christian right ministries placed full-page advertisements in newspapers across the United States offering services to "cure" homosexuals. Providing a message of love and hope for those deemed suffering, they are also the supporters of a bill in Congress that would ban federal housing funds to cities that require firms to provide domestic partnership benefits to their employees, including same-sex couples. The *New York Times* offers frequent reports on same-sex couples losing custody of their children, of gay men and women being thrown out of the military, and of legislation that curtails the rights of homosexuals. It is prudent to ask, therefore: after decades of fighting for sexual and gender rights, why is this backlash still occurring? Although the advertisements promising cures for homosexuals drew little response, they did receive widespread media attention that included an edition of the prime-time news magazine *Nightline*.

Representing the gay community was Andrew Sullivan, at that time editor of *The New Republic* and a conservative Republican. While declaring his full support for the ministries' first amendment rights, Sullivan explained his opposition to the ministries' practices by asserting that homosexuals have no more choice in their orientation than those born into a race category have about their racial group.

This dialog between political conservatives, played out in the mainstream media, claimed to include queer viewpoints, raising many questions concerning ongoing debates in queer communities. Should queer political energy be focused on deflecting challenges presented by right-wing fringe groups? Or should the agenda be a broader-based initiative of expanding rights while effecting wider social change? Are sexual and gender orientation innate, fundamental, and incorruptible, or is psychosocial and unconscious choice a factor? Moreover, what are the strategic ways to confront hidden prejudices reflected in religious "mouthtalk"? Is it strategically significant that a conservative Republican has been engaged to represent queer interests?

We note that we are living in a time when the gap between rich and poor is widening, where inequality and warfare are on the rise, where human needs are secondary to capitalist profit and accumulation, and where, finally, power is transnational and impersonal. Power and politics are central issues. But what kind of power, and what kind of politics? Members of queer communities exhibit confusion and ambivalence about these subjects. The managers of commodity production recognize that money speaks, and with a growing awareness that queer populations, or at least gay, white males, have in general more disposable income than other consumers, corporations and advertisers have been more than willing to orient their marketing campaigns to queer populations.

Temporary recognition and rights are granted when they produce profit, championed by those who understand the possibility of enhanced capitalist growth. But we know that rights will be just as fully opposed when the scape-goating of minority groups serves the same goal. The contradictions involved here are not entirely negative. The tolerance for diversity permitted by a growing economic arena does not automatically self-destruct when the productive realm weakens. Particularly for those with secure incomes not directly subject to the fluctuations of the market, the presented ideologies of fairness and justice may be kept long after general economic conditions have deteriorated.

Thus gains have not been quick to dissolve. An insistence on inclusion and equality by queer communities has succeeded in keeping crucial discussions alive. Changes have indeed come: from the continuing development of queer political organization that results in demands for recognition; from the alliances forged in reaction to the AIDS pandemic; and from the energy created by twenty-five years of a movement symbolically marked by the Stonewall uprising.

The politics of these movements, while not claiming to challenge or radically overturn the dominant structures of power, and despite conservative backlashes, did manage to transform the public sphere. The general population and the wider culture no longer automatically condemn queer lifestyles. Despite what "family-valued" conservatives continue to tell us, the National Gay and Lesbian Task Force reports that most Americans now support equality for homosexuals.[1] Certainly in urban areas there is a growing acceptance of queer lifestyles and, in a few, even an acceptance of equal rights. Given these gains, it would be difficult to assert that these movements were insignificant. The question of what we can learn from them remains.

As Foucault (1980) rightly observed, discriminatory labels are vehicles for the construction of alliances that can serve as a basis for liberation. But we also know that there are other forces at play, including the purveyors of ruling ideologies to suppress or involute liberatory energy before and as it occurs.[2] The many displays of homophobia by the Christian right, for example, correspond to an economy that we are told is in full swing, but which in fact has produced lower standards of living for most Americans – and a dearth of jobs with livable wages. The need for social control is reflected in the State's dialog with the extreme right, and in its record of backtracking on promises made to minority groups, including queer communities. The most notorious is perhaps President Clinton's inaugural campaign promise regarding the acceptance of gays in the military. These facts raise the specter that some of the blame may be with the tactics that queer communities have used to gain political ground. Is it possible that we are foreshadowing disappointment by working within the framework of accepted political norms?

The struggles for recognition and inclusion have their roots in the new social movements that began in the 1960s, in what Eder (1993) has referred to as "a new politics of class." Despite the differences and arguments that beset them, these movements and alliances resulted in the vast social scope and concern that is now labeled "diversity."

The Reagan years worked to disenfranchise these movements, not by disqualifying them but by usurping their energy. The Reagan administration's brilliance was its ability to redirect widespread discontent towards conservative goals. Rhetoric provided answers to the problems faced by many by proposing simple changes in attitude. The "breakdown of family values" became a metaphor for the existent problems of communities, violence, drug use, and even the exclusion of minorities from access to the basic tools for living. We were told that by repairing our thinking, we could also stimulate the economy by cutting social programs, somehow making life better for all.

## What then of theory?

What is the role of intellectuals in the building of emancipatory social movements? What do we mean when we call for equality? These questions have been asked, predominately, on college campuses and in classrooms. With students continuing to demand more accountability for the relevance of their studies, we have witnessed the birth of ethnic and identity studies, disciplinary concentrations in human rights, and a challenge to what we take for granted as cultural norms. In response to calls for inclusion, identity studies have become a mainstay in college curriculums. As part of this development – and as a reaction to it – what has thus evolved is a body of theory that is now known as "Queer."[3] However, unlike its predecessors in identity and ethnic studies, and despite the new social movements from which it evolved, "Queer theory" does not promote a real public engagement or a questioning of its tenets. Indeed, I will argue that Queer theory's highlighting of the impossibility of identity and the relativity of experience closely follows the development of current capitalist relations of production, where the self-contained individual is central to the economic goal of creating profit through production and its by-product, consuming. I will maintain that even the "newness" of Queer theory is not new, but has precursors in past theoretical debates, and that the hunger for novelty is the academic corollary to the drive for replacement labor and products by which capitalist relations of production attempt to create ongoing growth. It is thus my view that the tenets of Queer theory closely pattern the characteristics of social relations that it claims to reject. Rather than building resistance to the capitalist production of inequality, it has, paradoxically, mirrored it.

My intention, then, is to refocus current debates about a "queering of culture" to a level of analysis that includes social movements, race and class, power and dominance, and ultimately, social change. To do this, it is necessary to look historically and anthropologically at the world in which we live and the forces that affect our everyday lives. We should revisit the discussions concerning the relationship of economics to social being, to individual and social reproduction, and explore the way that "queer theorists" have used or ignored these concepts in their own work. Doing so provides both a critique and a synthesis that I hope can serve as a basis for furthering a discussion of theory, methodology, and practice.

## Examining Queer theory

We start with the premise that all social analyses are, perforce, political. We live in a political world ruled by forces that are opportunistic in nature, and driven towards the maintenance of dominance that has as its goal the accumulation of wealth. As such, our work is subsumed under an infrastructure of capitalism that has specific goals not tied to human social needs beyond the reproduction of labor. The analyses that we choose to pursue are a reflection of our relationship to this dominant economic nexus and our willingness or refusal to oppose it or deny its presence.

This assertion of choice, conscious or not, has an impact on the way we look at queer communities, arguments about biological components, and the social construction of gender and sexuality, including implicit assumptions about human nature.

Behavioral and psychological phenomena are a part of this process. Our beliefs about ourselves, the ways in which we act, our ability to express ourselves, and the behaviors we exhibit all play out within the limits of our experience and our ability to adapt to our surroundings. This may seem too obvious to the reader. But many of the dominant strands of current Queer theory, such as the signification of the self, the concentration on performativity (Butler, 1992), and the deconstruction of roles and identities pose the danger of forgetting that observable norms do exist, are enforced through socialization, and are fundamental to the exercise of power. In the realm of "performed" individuality, there is *no* identity. In fact, I will argue that these norms are all thoroughly informed by the persisting ego in the "individual's era" of capitalism. This level of analysis does not provide a means to analyze and to manage the alienation that capitalism produces because it codifies such differences into arguments about theory, rather than grounding them in society and history.

We thus require data on observable behavior. As Ruth Benedict succinctly summed up, "you cannot beat your culture." [4] For the study of gender, sexuality, and queer movements, the attentive analysis of the socio-political context is both necessary and primary. Whether we argue that sexuality and gender are social constructions or biological in nature, or both, it exists within a shared system of meanings and behaviors. This has often been forgotten in the current social context of theory that has led to analyses of social life, difference, and debates taking place within narrow academic frameworks.

## The postmodern turn

### Postmodernity and postmodernism

Queer theory stems from the movement in theory towards postmodernism and post-structuralism that developed in the 1970s and 1980s, and which has taken up residence in the halls of humanities and social science departments, even making forays into the empirical worlds of the natural sciences. How this shift from "modern" to "postmodern" and beyond occurred is the object of much disagreement, encompassing radically different views of the social and its consequences for the everyday life of individuals. [5]

The "post" of postmodernism presupposes a concept of something after, something beyond what has already been experienced or accomplished. It is both a theoretical and a historical category. It is the juncture of these two contexts to which postmodernism and post-structuralism have come to give meaning for the present project.

"Modernism" is derived from "modernity," that historical period of the Enlightenment where norms of reason, origins, and the search, later, for empirical validation took place. It was a reaction to the humanism of the Renaissance that emerged in the thirteenth century and an adaptation to the changes that took place with a transformation of social reproduction. [6] From the period of the Enlightenment we have the beginnings of ideology and from ideology, state rationalization and social control, viewed as parts of a larger concept of "progress." But we need to remember that the Enlightenment also corresponded to the development of capitalism in Europe. It was indeed a period of rapid social change: structures of the family, notions of the individual, and definitions of the "social" all were transformed, debated, and reconstituted by intellectual and political forces. There was no standard agreement here, for its leaders – from Rousseau to Condillac to the later romantics – all had their own visions of what it meant to be human, sometimes even arguing against their own work. Reason is easily generated to improve managerial styles and to better control aspects of work and daily life; rationalization is intertwined with directed activity. [7]

The reasoned logic of the Enlightenment was offset by the spiritual focus of its antagonists. These points of view have their own historical projectories and involve ongoing debates about the influence of, in particular, Immanuel Kant, Georg Hegel, and Friedrich Nietzsche. They are also contextualized within their own political and social frameworks: the French Revolution destroyed the basis for feudal obligations; the German movements against Enlightenment ideas were in the context of calls for separate identities within the Prussian Empire and the struggles for power that ensued.

The periods of the Enlightenment and counter-Enlightenment were followed in the nineteenth and twentieth centuries by an increased emphasis on empiricism and *managerial* rationality, corresponding again to currents of capitalist growth. The theories that grew out of this period, from Lenin to liberal economics to Rostow (1960), were still primarily based on a concept of modernity, the embodiment of the Enlightenment.

What then of "postmodernity"? It is a new period, tied to the growth of the world system, where differences in social organization render "objectivity" a problem. Cultures differ from one another, knowledge taken for granted becomes questionable. In a word, reality somehow is *destabilized*.

But are the historical periods and their cultural reflections necessarily given? Terry Eagleton (1997), making a distinction between the historical period of "postmodernity" and a culture of "postmodernism," tells us that "postmodernity"

> has real material conditions: it springs from an historic ephemeral, decentralized world of technology, consumerism and the culture industry, in which the service, finance and information industries triumph over traditional manufacture, and classical class politics yield ground to a diffuse range of "identity politics". Postmodernism is a style of culture which reflects something of this epochal change, in a depthless, decentered, ungrounded, self-reflexive, playful, derivative, eclectic pluralistic art which blurs the boundaries between "high" and "popular" culture, as well as between art and every-day experience.
>
> (Eagleton, 1997: vii)

Postmodernity and postmodernism, then, are not the same: while the analysis of "postmodernity" can be tied to actual historical junctures, the "postmodern" is only one idea that expresses that reality. Postmodern writers, then, confronting an increasingly fragmented and purposefully divided society, have devised a theoretical framework to incorporate the pieces. Perhaps it is a more linear logic than self-identified postmodernists would care to discuss. But it is assuredly *purposefully divided*, for the current fragmentation we witness and experience is not a result of a unilineal or "natural" evolution of society. It is a product of battles and junctures that have set the stage for what is now called late capitalism (Mandel, 1972).

## Michel Foucault and postmodernist theory

From a viewpoint of epistemology, much of the social theory of that developed in the 1970s and 1980s owes its lineage to Michel Foucault, whose *The Archaeology of Knowledge* (1972), *History of Sexuality* (1990), *Discipline and Punish* (1995), and the essays collected in *Power and Knowledge* (1980), began a refocusing of theory while sparking new concepts of power and ideology. That Foucault analyzed two important and ignored aspects of social functioning, sexuality and the penal system, contributed to his popularity as a social theorist. Particularly in the arena of sexuality and gender, scholars were ripe for a viewpoint that did not simply repeat a static rendering of sexuality as practice, or an essentialist, biological view of sexual functioning.

Beyond specific analyses of social institutions, Foucault's project aimed to rethink the ideas of power, ideology, and knowledge. Finding his own work inconclusive, he nevertheless believed that a substantial critique of existing concepts would yield a more precise understanding of subjugated "knowledges" that had not been previously recognized (1980: 78–80). Calling them "low-ranking" or "disqualified" knowledges (and using as examples the knowledge of the ill person, the patient, or the delinquent), what Foucault endeavored to show was that these forms of popular thought were subjugated by powerful opposing forces that rendered them nameless. Local knowledge, therefore, easily fell into "disuse" when confronted with more powerful dominators (1980: 82). Domination, however, swings like a pendulum: it changes over time and by the institutions and mechanisms that enforce social energies and control. Foucault's use of the concept of power ranges from the power of one knowledge to dominate another to the control over goods and wealth (1980: 78–108). It corresponds to what Eric Wolf (1999) called a "fourth modality of power," which was, for him,

> the power manifest in relationships that not only operates within settings and domains but also organizes and orchestrates the settings themselves, and that specifies the direction and distribution of energy flows. In Marxian terms, this refers to the power to deploy and allocate social labor ... it is ... the modality of power addressed by Michel Foucault when he spoke of "govern-ance," to mean the exercise of "action upon action." Marx addressed the structural relations of power between a class of capitalists and a class of workers, while Foucault was concerned rather with the structural relations that govern "consciousness."[8]

> (Wolf, 1999: 6)

For Foucault, then, governance is situational, driven by changing regimes of knowledge and their arenas (1980: 112). In other words, power involves shifts in the signification of regimes, or the creation of "truth," embodied by individuals. In his words, "The individual which power has constituted is at the same time its vehicle" (1980: 98).[9] It is this aspect of the individual as the embodiment and purveyor of power that Foucault alleges is ignored by Marx and his followers, who, he believed, posed the economic as separate and determinate, structurally composed by ideology, superstructures, and infrastructures (1980: 116). He therefore rejected the idea of a constituted *subject*, a static entity – the human, the individual – and the object – that of an institution, madness, the penal system or the like – that can be traced and constructed through and by history. Foucault instead preferred to employ a notion of *genealogy*, or

> a form of history which can account for the constitution of knowledges, discourses, domains of objects, etc. without having to make reference to a subject which is either transcendental in relation to the field of events or runs in its empty sadness throughout the course of history.
>
> (1980: 117)

Analyzing power through relations of consciousness, or perhaps more specifically through cultural flows that affect the way in which we experience and view the world, makes any concept of ideology too ambiguous to be of use in social analyses. Ideology becomes the outcome rather than a driver of social thought, the rationale behind power once it has been established. Power is what provides the basis for war and peace. Through disciplinary actions and punishment, a normalization of social functioning occurs that, in turn, dictates the constitution of the individual (cf. Foucault, 1995: 135–170). It is not, as Gramsci (1971) would have it, a purveyor of social stasis, but simply the rationale behind any set of ideas. Any use of a concept of ideology, then, is an afterthought, for ideology plays a role in the formation and justification of any idea or set of ideas. As Foucault concludes, ideology is

> difficult to make use of, for three reasons. The first is that like it or not, it always stands in virtual opposition to something else which is supposed to count as truth ... The second drawback is that the concept of ideology refers, I think necessarily, to something of the order of a subject. Thirdly, ideology stands in a secondary position to something which functions as its infrastructure, as its material, economic determinant, etc.
>
> (Foucault, 1980: 118)

What functions more effectively than a superstructural inclusion of ideology is "truth," defined as "a system of ordered procedures for the production, regulation, distribution, circulation and operation of statements" (1980: 133).

The argument that social systems are dictated through discourses of knowledge and enforcement leaves aside the mechanics of these regimes. Can ideology be extracted from the production of normalization in the social sphere? Is the constitution of normalization only found in the disciplinary functions of institutions that enforce dominant modes of behavior? Foucault believed that power is in fact a relation of continuing warfare, between and among regimes of power, social forces, and the individual (cf. Foucault, 1980: 102–116). But we would then have to assume that the individual has a resistant consciousness opposed to this regulation, but forced to concede to its domination. Discipline enforces behavior, the codes of social functioning – and here he uses the example of the Napoleonic Code – the mechanisms of control.

We can ask: if the subject becomes passive, then what happens to the construction of action that breaks the hold of disciplinary power? The individual and social action is rendered indiscernible. Knowledge is not accompanied by individual agency, but by enforceable practices, which swing through the evolution of time, but without an analysis of how power shifts have occurred.

In a similar manner, sovereignty is defined by Foucault as "something which refers to the displacement and appropriation on the part of power, not of time and labor, but of goods and wealth" (1980: 104). Power here becomes anthropomorphized, taking on a life and personality of its own. For how can goods and wealth be appropriated without a consideration of what produced them, that is, time and labor? This separation of labor from the sphere of reproduction is where Foucault radically breaks from Marx, who saw the connection of production, exchange, circulation, and consumption as part of the same process of social functioning.

Foucault therefore concludes that power

> is not primarily the maintenance and reproduction of economic relations, but is above all the relation of force ... power is essentially that which represses. Power represses nature, the instincts, a class, individuals ... so should not the analysis of power be first and foremost the analysis of repression?
>
> (Foucault, 1980: 90)

Clifford Geertz, in his *Local Knowledge* (1983), has elaborated on the importance of situated knowledge, and I have commented on the importance of "native points of view," particularly in the contexts of medicine and community development (Kirsch, 1998; Nash and Kirsch, 1988). In theory, these units of analysis could encompass Foucault's view of knowledge as determined by his notion of power. But this does not disqualify statements about the world in which local and native knowledge operate, or the development of that knowledge outside of dominant power structures. Local knowledge is often used to counter co-optation and of any understanding of "truth" and "reality" as they are presented to us. As forms of resistance, these knowledges pose challenges to dominant power structures. Local knowledges do not fall into "disuse" as Foucault would have it (1980: 82). They are the basis for community history, the checks for lived experience. Not only the "historical knowledge of struggles" (Foucault, 1980: 83), they are the basis for ongoing resistance, the embodiment of agency that characterizes human history.

The questions that Foucault raises about agency pose serious problems for an analysis of the political. First, "nature," "instincts," and "classes," which Foucault lumps together as unworthy of attention (1980: 91), are not simply abstractions. To talk of "instincts," for example, poses another grand narrative that has been aptly adopted by, for example, sociobiologists. Further, why should power necessarily be analyzed in the context of repression? Foucault uses repression in the names of Hegel, Freud, and Reich (1980: 90), but if we proceed beyond the philosophical or psychological level and confront the political as collective action, does it not make more sense to view power as a mechanism rather than a driver of social control? Which is to say that dominant ideologies cannot be narrowly defined as by-products of ideas and knowledge, but that they are the way in which we become convinced that the state is proceeding in the best interests of the people, realizing our needs.

Why not imagine that ideology, as social, is significantly more complex, inhabiting the many levels of the individual and the social that comprise both our bodies and society? The course of research that Foucault suggests imagines that power works against *something*, mostly the personal.

Oddly enough, Foucault's discussion around power seems to traverse back to the questions of human nature. As Rabinow sees it, Foucault avoids the question of the existence of human nature, while researching its function in society: "He doesn't refute them; instead, his consistent response is to historicize grand abstractions. In the last analysis, he does not take a stand on whether or not there is a human nature" (Rabinow, 1984: 4). Even so, the work indicates a concept of nature that involves a pessimistic struggle over the gaining and losing of power, accomplished through the discourse that is subject of Foucault's work. We are left with specific historical examples, such as the medical canon or the penal system as tools of social control, but we do not have a comprehensive analysis of how they came to serve this position.

## From class to discourse

In France, the tide of postmodernism took its deciding turn after the events of 1968. As Gordon (in Foucault, 1980) reflects, Marxism had held a place of eminence in European universities, often equating the theories of Marx with the reality of the so-called "socialism" evidenced by the Soviet bloc. The failure of the movements of 1968 to achieve basic change in capitalist relations and the obvious problems of inequality, the continued co-optation of the left, and social oppression within the Soviet Union led many to perceive that the left had been defeated, and questioned the usefulness of Marxism as a tool for change that united theory and practice and the social and the individual.[10]

When the collective as political did not suffice, the personal as political took hold. Shadowing this development was the questioning of *labor* as the starting point of analysis for social reproduction. Labor movements had failed to make significant differences in the inclusion of suppressed voices, both in their internal organizations and at a societal level. This failure began to be conceived as a problem not only with labor movements but also with the theories that elevated labor to the structural basis for revolution. If theory, in the name of the "modern," had failed to provide adequate methodologies for solving the problems of inequality and exploitation, it was reasoned, then the basis of individual experience and social reproduction needed to be reconceptualized.

As an alternate view, *discourse* began to take on importance as a way of examining forces of domination and the regulation of knowledge. Foucault, in *The Archaeology of Knowledge* (1972), presented discourse as a way of describing social interaction and regulation, posing *language* as the grounds by which processes of thought and knowledge are derived, the way in which *discursive formations* order human experience. Thus, the subject, say "tradition" (1972: 21), is dismissed as an object of analysis; for the subject, or subjectivity, itself is a result of a discursive formation, embodied by individuals but which includes aspects of individual experience as well as excludes them.[11]

Foucault here is not claiming new categories, for discourses themselves are a result of other discourses. In his words,

> these divisions – whether our own, or those contemporary with the discourse under examination – are always themselves reflexive categories, principles of classification, normative rules, institutionalized types: they, in turn, are facts of discourse that deserve to be analyzed beside others; of course, they also have complex relations with each other, but they are not intrinsic, autochthonous, and universally recognizable characteristics.
>
> (1972: 22)

The formulation of discourse rids any discussion of given categories. Historical analyses become synchronic by nature; they do not include *the past* but rather the discursive formations present in a historical period. There is, then, an objection to any notion of origins as posed by an anthropological methodology (1972: 14), or the totality of cultural categories such as "world-views, ideal types, the particular spirit of an age" (1972:14–15).

It was not Foucault's project to establish the validity of this method. Indeed, he admits to having been prone to the same mistakes of cultural totalizing that he is critiquing (1972: 17). He is cautious about claiming methodological superiority, making sure that the reader is aware of his ambivalence:

Hence the cautious, stumbling manner of this text: at every turn, it stands back, measures up what is before it, gropes towards its limits, stumbles against what it does not mean, and digs pits to mark out its own path. At every turn, it denounces any possible confusion. It rejects its identity, without previously stating: I am neither this nor that. It is not critical, most of the time; it is not a way of saying that everyone else is wrong. It is an attempt to define a particular site by the exteriority of its vicinity; rather than trying to reduce others to silence, by claiming that what they say is worthless, I have tried to define this blank space from which I speak, and which is slowly taking shape in a discourse that I still feel to be so precarious and unsure.

(1972: 17)

It is this act of disclaiming that differentiates Foucault's method from those that came before him. By disclaiming relevance, there is no requirement to conjoin a course of action with the application of the method.

The broad influence of this reworking of analytic thought finds its way into a critique of the "fetishism of labor" with Baudrillard's *Mirror of Production* (1975), where the entire concept of production as a basis for social reproduction is critiqued. For Baudrillard, the "code" of social life provides the meaning for commodities and consumption, not the act of labor that Marx argued the commodity embodies. The code defines who speaks and who does not, who is heard and who is silenced. Production becomes a discourse – in his words, "a productivist discourse" (1975: 18) – like all others; it is signified by the code that embraces it, the "dominant scheme" that determines its definition.

Baudrillard makes an analogy to the way in which people view themselves in contemporary culture, as products of what they do: we are taught to believe that we are what we achieve, and achievement is an end result of what we produce. Using the analogy of Lacan's "mirror stage," where the outside is reflected into consciousness, he concludes that "Production, labor, value, everything in which an objective emerges and through which an objective world emerges and through which man recognizes himself objectively – this is the imaginary" (1975: 19). Production is rejected as a starting point for investigating social systems, from pre-capitalist "primitive" formations to those of the present. To prove his point, Baudrillard – unfairly – accuses the French anthropologist Maurice Godelier of superimposing categories of production onto pre-capitalist societies, just as he accuses Marx of reifying production and need as basic to human existence.[12]

From Foucault and Baudrillard we see the development of a turn from "objective" circumstances to self-reflection. Perhaps it can be implied that the failures of 1968 generated this self-reflection, not in the political arena of action and program but in the doubting of all that can be called "truth." Self-reflection involves our consciousness and an ability to define activity. However, if we do not believe in truth, then we cannot fail.

For both Foucault and Baudrillard, this self-reflection is then superimposed onto previous "categories" of grand schemes and meta-narratives, which are dismissed along with the universalism of the modernist period, a universalism, as found in Marx, that did not achieve the liberation of its subjects, or peoples.[13]

With the dismissal of categories, universal subjects, and through-lines of history comes the objective problem of class. Because Marx has misinterpreted primitive, archaic, and feudal modes of production by superimposing universal categories onto them, he has also misinterpreted capitalism (Baudrillard, 1975: 107). Historical materialism thus suffers from a basic methodological weakness. For

> not only have the categories of historical materialism no meaning outside our own society, but *perhaps in a fundamental way they no longer have any meaning for us* [italics in the original] ... Historical materialism prohibits itself from seeing this. It is incapable of thinking the process of ideology, of culture, of language, of the symbolic in general. It misses the point not only with regard to primitive societies, but it also fails to account for the radicality of the separation in our societies, and therefore the radicality of the subversion that grows there.
>
> (1975: 109)

If class is simply the by-product of an elusive category of capital, then as a category in itself it has little meaning. It is a "universalist and rationalist concept," and Baudrillard tells us that "When the structure is reversed and the proletarian class triumphs, as in the East, nothing changes profoundly, as we know, in social relations" (1975: 168). The radicality of separation and subversion must come from other sources, in the reaction and subversion of the "codes" that are superimposed onto the individual.[14] Collective action, one would assume, would need to arise from a unitary rejection of these codes, a spontaneous response for which no one can be said to be responsible.

Foucault and Baudrillard both find power in the spoken word that regulates social activity. The analysis is linguistic rather than materialistic, a reductionism that Bloch has brilliantly summarized in his own analysis of the genesis of knowledge (Bloch, 1997). This reorientation from Marx is perhaps what best defines the political aspect of postmodernism and post-structuralism. Although, as Poster (1989) argues, Foucault and Baudrillard, as well as Derrida, Barthes, Lacan, Lyotard, and Deleuze – the most widely recognized of the postmodern and post-structuralist theorists – have all participated in the politics of the left, it is perhaps this very involvement that has demoralized their sense of struggle. For all of them, Marxist theory, and by association modern social theory in general, did not adequately stimulate emancipation. The conclusion is that emancipation must come from within, and the within is constituted by language.[15]

### Postmodernism and post-structuralism

Most current postmodern theory is accomplished without the benefit of the inclusion of a material analysis of *postmodernity* that would clearly position its genesis. Without this analysis, we are left to imagine that these are novel and even radical reinterpretations of present-day culture. It is, these writers say, their task to go beyond the observable to a reality of pieces that can be further taken apart. The basic tenet of postmodernism and of post structuralism is this destabilization through deconstruction.

The difference between the postmodern and post-structuralist positions is, Rosenau suggests, more methodological than interpretive in practice: they are

> not identical, they overlap considerably and are sometimes considered syn-
> onymous. Few efforts have been made to distinguish between the two,
> probably because the differences appear to be of little consequence ... the
> major difference is one of emphasis more than substance. Postmodernists are
> more oriented towards cultural critique while the poststructuralists empha-
> size method and epistemological matters.
>
> (Rosenau, 1992: 13)

Structuralism, according to its critics, poses binary oppositions and structures of social life that exclude the possibility of variants. It is most apparent in the works of Saussure, who posed a binary structure of language – the signifier and the signified – and the need to separate *langue* and *parole*, or synchrony from diachrony (Timpanaro, 1970: 135–219). It is also evident in the corpus of works by Claude Lévi-Strauss, who analyzed structures of kinship and exchange to des-cribe relationships among communities. Steven Seidman, pointing to structuralist thought in the context of cultural studies, refers to structuralism as an idealist reductionism of the relationship between culture and society (1997: 64–65).

Thus, reacting to another "kind of universal logic that appears to structure human relations" (Butler, 1990: 39), the post-structuralists break with structural-ist premises by refuting

> the claims of totality and universality and the presumption of binary structural
> oppositions that implicitly operate to quell the insistent ambiguity and open-
> ness of linguistic and cultural signification. As a result, the discrepancy be-
> tween signifier and signified becomes the operative and limitless *différence* of
> language, rendering all referentiality into a potentially limitless displacement.
>
> (Butler, 1990: 40)

Along with Foucault, post-structuralist thought is most often associated with Jacques Derrida, who uses *text* rather than behavior to explicate meaning. Text in our present culture, he asserts, is the driving force of meaning, an arena of imbedded symbols that are neither completely understood by the reader nor intended by the author. Because text is variable by interpreter, there can be no closure or agreement in understanding among individuals in society. Language in this way is taken out of its social context, it becomes "pre-discursive." The reader is unaware and the author is absent – the ideas relayed are still present, but connect somewhere in the unconscious realm (a description that would be debated) in the reader's mind. Language and text become a series of encoded meanings provided by the symbols of words and their interrelations.

But language, of course, is the ultimate social phenomenon. Symbols can take on many meanings to many people; they can be incorporated into existing systems of thought and transformed – that is to say, changed. They can have meanings to individuals and cultures that are beyond what may be understood by their authors or deconstructors, and they can be used in the process of ideological creation both to support and to resist modes of domination. We only have to note the resurgence of previously outcast languages such as Welsh, as one example, to see that symbols have political content. It is the same linguistic reductionism that the post-structuralists accuse structuralist writers of projecting that makes it difficult to examine fully the content of history and politics, for the designation of text as containers of pre-discursive activity fails to fully analyze the very symbols it projects.

By taking language and text as a starting point, then, the person and individual as subject remain absent and unexplored, and agency becomes a moot point. Even consciousness is not an object of analysis, but it is indeed imbedded in the text itself. But if the individual does not exist, where is the "self" so often presented? The individual must then be present and absent at the same time. The physical body becomes an object of text rather than a recognizable form. In dismissing the individual in name if not in fact, postmodernism and post-structuralism have indeed reified the "idea" of the individual, without an identity. The individual is, then, replaced by "mind." It is the mind that serves as the site of experience and interprets it; but the interpretation can only be *read* as text. It cannot be acted upon. I assume here that the "individual" is a central unit of analysis for postmodernists and post-structuralists, even if the person as subject is dismissed. They refer to a separate self whenever they refer to an "I" or to "experience." These can only pertain to individual human beings.

Postmodern theorists deconstruct and dismiss the empirical. But unlike other critics of empiricism they do not attempt to reconstruct a logic that could represent phenomena of daily life; they are against any form of representation, believing the search for "truth" is impossible. But as Rosenau also notes,

> If post-modernists were consistent and true to the linguistic relativism they expound, and if they really believed successful communication was impossible,

they would cease to deconstruct what others wrote or said. To avoid being hypocritical, they would have to remain silent [Weber, 1990: 143]. If post-modernists were sincere when they stated that no statements are privileged, not even their own, then they would have to give up their right to speak with authority. Only this would assure internal consistency.

(Rosenau, 1992: 178)

But consistency and truth are not the only points of contention here. The consequences of this theory for politics and the building of alliances has major repercussions for any current analysis of social change.

## The academic context

Queer theory emerged within an institutional context where radical social critiques have become passé. This is in part due to popular attacks on the academy, which have portrayed colleges and universities as enclaves promoting elitist conceptions and students who are, at best, unmarketable, but it is also a result of the present conservatism in the culture at large.

Particularly in the liberal arts, the idea of the academic world as a practical endeavor has seemed to some to be something of an oxymoron. Liberal ed-ucation, for many, is no longer regarded as a stepping-stone to career objectives or a practical tool for social integration. Administratively, student loans and grants have been eroded, reinforcing the notion that quality education is a luxury of the rich. As a consequence, the gap in educational opportunities between rich and poor has become ever more evident (see Jacoby, 1994). In the United States, at least, the need for higher education is upheld on one level, while on another, attacks are played out in popular culture with media spins asserting that colleges are overcharging the public and that the employees of higher education are simply intellectuals involved in meaningless debates of their own making. To be sure, the disintegration of social programs has also meant the erosion of public primary and secondary schools, but nowhere is the wrath of education critics directed more than toward the halls of university campuses.

Despite the obvious reasons for the prominence of this ideology – the desire for federal and state governments to find places to cut budgets, the rising costs of many private universities, and the perceived lack of specific skills produced by a liberal arts education – the academy has not directly entered into the debate. It has, in fact, progressively separated itself from applied concerns. In like form, academic theory applicable to the many social issues confronting world societies has not succeeded in convincing the public, or university administrations for that matter, that the attack needs to be challenged. While the political right takes over the White House, as Todd Gitlin notes, academics have been busy marching on English departments (Gitlin, 1995: 126–159). While governments and funders find more reasons to deconstruct institutions, the academy has been blind to the need for addressing popular belief about the realities of academic life, constructing barriers that reinforce the "elitism" that academia projects in public thought.

Part of academia's conforming to popular pressure in this way stems from the competition resulting from decreasing budgets and the need to prove *internal* worthiness. Creativity itself has become a matter of competition. There are fewer jobs available, and fewer still come with the security offered by tenure and chairs. There has developed a culture of novelty where in order to secure a position one needs to offer something new, preferably without any aspect of controversy. While race, sex, gender, and class have become buzzwords in the university setting, it is infinitely less dangerous to use them within the contexts of theory than it is to take on the foundations of the larger socio-political structure. Similarly, it is certainly safer to *deconstruct* theories of social being than to *construct* modes of social action.

# 2 Making Queer theory

In every epoch the ideas of the ruling class are the ruling ideas, that is, the class that is the ruling material power of society is at the same time its ruling intellectual power.

(Karl Marx, "Ideology in General, Especially German Philosophy")

You cry, but you endanger nothing in yourself. It's like the idea of crying when you do it. Or the idea of love.

("Prior to Louis," Angels in America, part 2, Kushner, 1995)

Queer theory developed as a course of inquiry within the past decade. From modest beginnings in the academic realms of literature and philosophy, recent writings now specifically target the social sciences and even the medical canon as areas for the reinterpretations of assumed concepts.

The outcome of these writings for social action and social change remains to be adequately evaluated. In the temptation to be new, so important in academic society and in American culture, the area of Queer theory has taken on meaning without specific objectives or goals. In the rush of enthusiasm to establish new academic and popular boundaries, the focus of this theory has been loosely directed at showing how and why traditional disciplinary expositions have failed to do justice to queer populations. Yet very few careful analyses have examined the effects and influences of these queer viewpoints on existing academic disciplines, or, perhaps more importantly, in the context of modern social life.

## Beginnings

The beginnings of Queer theory are anchored to the post-1960's disengagement with organizational left politics and the reaction to the then current politics of "the left" in its entirety. If, as we have seen, there was a belief that left politics was disenfranchised as a means for enacting social change, then the aim of "queer" was one of a resistance identity, in Castells' (1997) terms, while building the kind of "meta-identity" that is not limited by labels or social constructions.

What demarcates Queer theory from its postmodernist and post-structuralist foundations is its referral to a range of work "that seeks to place the question of sexuality as the centre of concern, and as the key category through which other social, political, and cultural phenomena are to be understood" (Edgar and Sedgwick, 1999: 321). Hogan and Hudson (1998) place the beginnings of a "Queer theory" with Teresa de Laurentis's use of the term for a 1989 conference at the University of California, Santa Cruz, and cite Eve Kosofsky Sedgwick's questioning of the *meaning* assumed in the binary definitions of sexuality in her *Between Men* (1985) and *Epistemology of the Closet* (1990) as the scholarly works most closely associated with its acceptance into academia (1998: 491).

The *principle* of "queer," then, is the disassembling of common beliefs about gender and sexuality, from their representation in film, literature, and music to their placement in the social and physical sciences. The *activity* of "queer" is the "queering" of culture, ranging from the reinterpretation of characters in novels and cinema to the deconstruction of historical analyses. As activity, we have seen the assertation of identity of "queers," notably held as lesbian, gay, transgender, bisexual, and transsexual, as variants of human behavior that have rights on their own terms. As *theory*, queer's derivation from postmodernism and post-structuralism leads to the rejection of all categorizations as limiting and labeled by dominant power structures.

In more popular terms, Queer Nation embraced "queer" in the late 1980s to signify a free-flowing organization of resistance that promised to transcend mainstream politics and include all who were against any set conceptions of gender, sexuality, and power. The organization rejected assimilation and identity, but ultimately it was these same questions of identity and action that pulled it apart. "Queer" has, nonetheless, become part of the popular lexicon among those who disclaim the dominance of heterosexuality, and "we're queer and we're here" has become the staple chant of any rally bringing together LGBT peoples and others.

The popular use of queer and the academic context of queer, then, do not coincide as much as they are both based on loose resistance strategies to sexual and gender labeling. Most activists involved in gay and lesbian and queer organizations have not read Queer theory, even if some of the more prominent scholars are recognizable names. Many also question the usefulness of this mode of disassembling and fear that it may be working against productive means by which self-actualization and organizational resistance is built (cf. Duberman, 1997).

Beyond small theatrical endeavors such as Queer Nation and Sex Panic, the arguments around Queer theory are firmly rooted within the halls of theoretical treatises where political movements and social action have traditionally taken a back seat to the explication of theory, leading Brett Beemyn and Mickey Eliason, for example, to wonder whether it is significant that "postmodern theory, which denies the reality of identity markers like gender, race, and sexuality, should emerge at the historic moment when the voices of previously marginalized groups are beginning to have some impact on the academy" (1996: 220).

Here lies the puzzle: if there are movements to institutionalize Queer theory and queer studies within academic settings, what characteristics of a discipline does it offer? Moreover, if "queer" is meant to be or become a basis for a social movement, then who defines it and who does the movement belong to? Who does it include? What is its foundation?

Many of those who identify themselves as Queer theorists would no doubt object to this attempt at narrowing the subject: they would argue that its broad sweep and encompassing constitution have quite enough justification to warrant the support of academic policy committees, and beyond the academy, the political arena.

What is queer in the public sphere is, with caveats, a "new" social movement. But most of the theoretical statements about the notion of "queer" have been made in the academy, and these have separated theory and action. It is my goal to show that theory has far-reaching consequences for social action, and I will continue to reflect on the development of theory that lies behind the notion of "queer," and its subsequent development.

## Queer theory proper

We know that Queer theorists object to statements that would construct boundaries. All would seem to agree, for example, that the traditional "heterosexual/homosexual" dichotomy should be abandoned, and that a third or more ways of describing and analyzing sex and gender should be proposed. For Annamarie Jagose, whose much cited *Queer Theory* (1998) has become an authoritative text on the genre, "queer is very much a category in the process of formation ... It is not simply that queer has yet to solidify and take on a more consistent profile, but rather that its definitional indeterminacy, its elasticity, is one of its constituent characteristics." Given this lack of definition, Jagose proposes that Queer assumes "'a zone of possibilities' ... always inflected by a sense of potentiality that it cannot yet quite articulate," and proposes that it "describes those gestures and analytical modes which dramatize incoherence in the allegedly stable relations between chromosomal sex, gender and sexual desire" (1998: 2–3). Other writers have gone further in emphasizing a refusal to take definitional stands. David Halperin, for example, suggests than even its designation is suspect, for "Once conjoined with 'theory,' ... 'queer' loses its offensive, vilifying tonality and subsides into a harmless generic qualifier, designating one of the multiple departments of academic theory" (1995: 32). His concern is that "the more it verges on becoming a normative academic discipline, the less Queer theory can plausibly claim to be" (1995: 113). There are also some that take the notion of queer outside of the limiting realm of gender and sexuality. Aaron Betsky, for one, explores "queer space" as a "misuse or deformation of a place, an appropriation of the buildings and codes of the city for perverse purposes" (1997: 5).

It is the belief of these writers that we should not attempt to integrate individual self-understanding and reflection into broader forms of identification. Even the relating of experience, as Joan Scott has it, is limited by who is doing the experiencing and by who is recording the experiencing. Those who try to use experience as the basis of inquiry "take as self-evident the identities of those whose experience is being documented and thus naturalize their difference" (1993: 399). In such a way, the mindful experiences of individual selves are not really explorable provinces.[1]

If indeterminacy is a basic tenet of those things queer, then the project of disassembling "norms" is the major goal. It is meaningful that just as the wave of postmodernism that hit the academic disciplines in the late 1970s and 1980s began to be discredited in the 1990s, post-structuralist thought surfaced to take its place.[2] The act of deconstruction, the basic tenet of post-structuralism, is more suitable to the act of disassembling than the broad statements that postmodern analysts generally make. It is a logical development, for deconstruction assumes that you can take apart categories rendering the constituent parts ambiguous.[3]

In this way, Queer theory becomes separate from past gay and lesbian politics by dismissing "gay" and "lesbian" as categories containing subjects, for asserting subjects automatically erases those who do not perfectly match. Indeed, Judith Butler warns that those who endeavor to resist the danger of public erasure must be careful not "to counter that violence [by installing] another in its place" (1991: 19).

In university settings these tenets of indeterminacy become more than elements of theory. Indeterminacy has become a fashion statement among faculty and students, for it can be worn as a motivational accessory without analytic reference to the texts that attempt to make the case. These writings need not be read and are rarely critically evaluated; nor are their implications for social life considered. It is, indeed, enchanting for those without a political program but who detect and wish to address, simply, the inequality that exists in everyday life. Queer theorists have succeeded in generating a following that sees postmodern and post-structuralist thought as a signifier of opposition to *something*, a comfortable if incomplete position of non-recognition and inaction.

## Queer theory and diversity

Whether "queer," "gay and lesbian," or neither, what these writers and activists have in common is their call for the acceptance of diversity. Diversity has become the benchmark of academic tolerance, the catch-all for policies that range from academic admissions and course offerings, to the distribution of positions and power within workplaces and within broader communities. Whether their ideas are taken to extremes (the stand that to identify *any* categories is an affront to the differences that constitute diversity), or more geared toward institutional policy reform, these theorists are trying to work against current cultural trends that attempt to assimilate all difference into an arena of ideal types suitable for social cohesion and control.

Diversity in Queer theory assumes the resistance to "normativity," and dominant cultural values. As we have seen, the use of "power" for Queer theorists is self-reflective: you can subvert its hegemony by refusing to conform to its practices. In so far as being political involves the exercise of power, individual action is political. It is subjective.

Ultimately, the confusion and entanglement that the category "queer" creates in academic circles is constituted with contradictions: while Queer theory supposes that categories and labels are to be ignored, it is still a deconstruction of existing categories of peoples and cultures. In one sense, it is simply a *reaction* to labeling, and on that level it is undefinable in relation to a purpose, for it does not propose a social alternative. The "we" of identification is omitted.

What is not addressed is the material reality that minorities are by definition part of the larger culture, labeled and determined by it. Like ethnicities, they act in tandem with dominant structures of power that militate against their full expression. Deconstructing categories of identity erases the specificity of the components of "queer," in the name of "queer is as queer is, or does."

The relative experience of queer peoples is comparable with all those who have been marginalized. While "queerness" cuts across class, status, and power, the interplay of scapegoating and rejection is performed in the same arena as the struggles against class oppression, racism, and sexism more broadly. In every case, the stigmatized group of individuals does not meet an ideal and suffers the consequence. When a society tells individuals that they are not meeting their potential as workers, fathers, wives, and sexual beings, then self-hatred is one response. Resentment and anger is another. The questions remain: what is the ideal, what is its purpose, and how does it differentially affect those who must confront it?

Western culture, and especially US culture, is deeply rooted in a model of the individual as primary actor and subject. As Arensberg (n.d.) demonstrated in his discussion of what we mean by "common sense," Americans, like many Western cultures, see status as the result of achievement, privilege and authority as "deserved," and "success" as a personal goal above all and an ethical imperative. Success is a result of self-motivation and access to resources is a result of individual effort.

Like other minorities and ethnic groups, workers, and the disenfranchised, queers are easily blamed when they "fail" to conform to a social ideal. Unlike the case of other minorities, however, the relative affluence of mainstream gay male and, to a lesser extent, lesbian communities often provides temporary opportunities for integration. Thus, the experience of the privileged gay or lesbian individual is necessarily distant from that of a colonial subject. But the distance can be illusory. In the grasp of this illusion, one can be led to believe that struggles shared with those having a common identity are not a basis for alliance. This was the case for the carefully closeted, and is the case for those who regard identity as superfluous. The illusion of safety is itself a condition of entitlement that is not held by those without it.

What does this mean for our current understanding of Queer theory and the future of its development? An epistemology of its intellectual trajectory is important in this discussion of theory and practice. We assume that developments in culture and society are connected to the intellectual production of knowledge. But what, we have to ask, is the basis for social change?

## Precursors

The debates concerning Queer theory have their antecedents. In the nineteenth century, Marx's arguments with the "Young Hegelians" foreshadowed the current debates around the refutation of political economy and the definition of the social, particularly in the discussion of experience and the derivation of consciousness.

Marx and Engels' writings on the Young Hegelians formed the basis for the "Theses on Feuerbach." While the intention of the Young Hegelians was to place the study of religion within historical inquiry and human motivation, Marx and Engels maintained that the resulting perspective placed the primacy of individuals and ideas over social activity.

The basis of the Young Hegelians' critique of German philosophy was religion and the role of the individual. The differences around the function of religion set the stage for the still lively debates around the derivation of consciousness. Marx and Engels disputed the idea that consciousness was derived from mental activity, which, they claimed, abstracted human beings from their contexts. They argued instead that the individual portrayed in classical German philosophy could only be understood by linking that person with his or her productive activity. Like many of today's Queer theorists, the Young Hegelians saw themselves as radical social critics, prompting Marx to remark:

> Let us teach man, says one person, to exchange these imaginings for thoughts that correspond to man's essence; let us teach man to be critical towards them, says another; let us teach man to get rid of them altogether, says a third. Then – existing reality will collapse.
>
> Such innocent and childlike fantasies make up the core of recent Young-Hegelian philosophy which not only is received with horror and awe by the

German public, but is also propounded by the *philosophic heroes* themselves with a ceremonious consciousness of its cataclysmic dangerousness and criminal disregard.

(Marx, 1967: 404)

Marx and Engels' aim was to elucidate how ideas are generated through the act of production and are actualized through the processes of daily activity. The Young Hegelians believed that consciousness could change the reality of people, that "all their actions, their chains, and their limitations are products of their conscious-ness" (Marx, 1967: 407).

The Young Hegelians' critique of German philosophy was seen by Marx and Engels, then, as essentially conservative. The Young Hegelians were not fighting against actual modes of inequality, they argued, but simply against certain ways of thinking about them:

Consequently they give men the moral postulate of exchanging their present consciousness for human, critical or egotistic consciousness to remove their limitations. This amounts to a demand to interpret what exists in a different way, that is, to recognize it by means of a different interpretation. The Young Hegelian ideologists are the staunchest conservatives, despite their allegedly "world-shaking" statements. The most recent among them have found the correct expression for their doings in saying that they are fighting only against "*phrases*." They forget, however, that they fight them only with phrases of their own. In no way are they attacking the actual existing world; they merely attack the phrases of this world.

(Marx, 1967: 408)

The positions presented by the Young Hegelians and present-day Queer theorists are not far apart. I will argue in the following pages that the historical echoing includes facing the same consequences as those posed by Marx and Engels: that we cannot change our position by simply changing ourselves. In their words, "Not one of these philosophers ever thought to look into the connection between German philosophy and German reality, between their criticism and their own material environment" (Marx, 1967: 409).

## Class in Queer theory

Class, like other categories of social construction, is not a central concern of Queer theory, outside of its reference as a "meta-narrative" or an essentialist proposition. While we can find references to "class" in the lists that include sex, gender, and race, there is no attempt in the writings of Queer theorists to use it as a social phenomenon. Indeed, none of the essays in Steven Seidman's collection of essays in *Queer Theory / Sociology* (1996) even refers to class beyond "middle" or "working." What is the meaning of class, then, for Queer theory?

For most Americans, at least, class is not easily identifiable. Raffo (1998) reports that in the 1992 presidential elections, 92 per cent of the voting population self-identified as "middle class."[4] Corresponding to an overriding trust that economic status is temporary and malleable and that mobility is the foundation of capitalist production, "middle" allows for an ambiguity that promises hope, neither opposing nor supporting the current forms of government. It is not a "bourgeois" class or a "merchant" class as Marx would have determined it, naming a group of people with a particular relation to the mode of production, but a more indeterminate kind of grouping. The indeterminacy of "middle" is supported by the folklore of the rags-to-riches stories that continue to be generated by the examples of the few who win the lottery, either figuratively or literally.

The post-war boom period of the 1950s and 1960s enhanced the credibility of these beliefs as upward mobility became a "natural" occurrence for many American families. The evidence that this mobility was relative to capitalist accumulation, and that wealth created in the West was achieved at the expense of other parts of the world, did not diminish the power of the idea that economic security was available to all. It could indeed be achieved by following some basic rules. In fact, however, such beliefs represent an adaptation to an ideal of economic security that rarely exists.[5] What happens in communities when even the appearance of the ideal is eroded is that sectors of those communities become, by the process of scapegoating, the focus of blame and of violence. Class origins and experience easily become translated as a part of culture, rather than any structural positioning of people to the rest of society.

Yet, there *is* a developing appreciation among exploited peoples that class and politics are truly part of both the personal and the political, and by extension the personal as political.[6] We experience class in relation to others, in our ability to gain status and to relate positively to structures of power. Because the ideology of capitalism also generates ideals that assume upward mobility and access to resources, there is a particular Western ideology that presumes that one's class can be changed by an act of will. More egregiously, it is thought by some not to exist at all. To identify oneself as "lower class" often includes an assumption that the goal of access is unattainable; at the same time, few not in real positions of power would self-identify as upper class. Class, then, as identified within popular culture, does not take on the characteristics of Marx's categories, which assume organization (Marx and Engels, 1959: 16; Moody, 1997: 145).

The meaning of class has undergone transformation with the theoretical trends that accompany its use, and, like race and gender, it is often given assumed meaning. It is likely to be confused with a Weberian notion of "status" – a position that can change over time and with differential resources that are reflected in employment position, immigration status, or age. The *experience* of class as status is expressed in many ways. It is about *consumption* rather than *production*, and the access to goods and services that consumption allows, as we shall see in Chapter 4. While some exercise control over others, indeed even participating in the consumption of others in the form of their labor, it is finally control over *production and its organization* that determines class.[7] On a personal level, then, class is contextual (Raffo, 1998: 6). On a structural level, however, it is not.

## Power and the production of ideology

Inequality is an outcome of particular social phenomena: it can be denied or asserted, analyzed or deconstructed, but any discussion of its presence or absence is played out in the *ideological* levels of our current social relations.

Ideology is at once a study of ideas and a rationalization for dominance. For Therborn (1980) ideology is not only "social cement."[8] For to define ideology as *only* the expression of ideas negates its purpose: in this context all ideas have expressions, strictly speaking, and therefore all are equivalent. But from its beginnings the notion of ideology has had political implications. The term dates to Destrutt de Tracy's proposal for a "science of ideas" (Thompson, 1990: 28) and it found its most fervent beginnings in the workings of the French Revolution. The calls for Liberty, Fraternity, and Equality were championed by indentured servants to promote the overthrow of a dominating state in crisis; but these ideas were also disseminated for the first time through a kind of mass media – pamphlets, circulars, and newspapers – that enabled messages to reach large audiences. The results of this new mode of struggle, paradoxically, also served another purpose: it allowed for the birth of capitalism in France. It freed peasants from their overlords, but it also contained its own dangers. In the French Revolution, "be careful what you wish for" took on real meaning for those who found themselves indeed free, but only to sell their labor for the wages of poverty. The French population became dependent on those who would hire them. They lost another kind of freedom, the land which had formed the basis for their communities.[9] As D'Emilio summarizes it, the development of capitalism freed us from

> the ownership of anything but our labor power ... we are also freed in the negative sense, from any other alternative. This dialectic – the constant interplay between exploitation and some measure of autonomy – informs all of the history of those who have lived under capitalism.
>
> (D'Emilio, 1997: 468)

Unlike Foucault's insistence that ideology is simply the realm of ideas (1980: 118), Thompson has more productively positioned ideology as "*meaning in the service of power*" (1990: 7). Ideologies represent powerful agendas. Furthermore, Leacock underscored ideology's historical relationship to a developing division of labor that requires mental work and planning to accomplish production and reproduction (Leacock, 1972: 66). Marx's oft-quoted declaration that the ruling ideas of an epoch are the ideas of the ruling class is, of course, still true today.[10] Dominant ideas are the building blocks of the ruling culture, and they encourage us to think, act, and believe in particular ways. Any attempt to counter these ideas takes place, by definition, in relation to their presence. Our project is therefore to find the subtext behind what will be "revealed if we can discover the nature of determinacy which non-ideas exert over ideas" (Hall, 1978: 10).

Social power is therefore presented through ideology, symbolism, and, finally, through force. Domination means the ability to define what things are and who they benefit. Power is a matter of relationships, including those between individuals, among corporations, and between communities and governments. Those who hold power have the means to define laws that legitimate rights and vested interests, and to perpetuate them. Furthermore, what is legally and morally binding from the perspective of those who hold power may well be an instrument of political oppression from the point of view of those who do not.

But once people are freed as individuals to face their own fate, the mechanisms of capitalism treat all alike as expendable workers and consumers. Its purpose, as Dalla Costa writes, is to render the "body as a mere container for labor power or a machine for reproducing labor power" (1996: 120). Taking this atomization to its logical next step, the body becomes saleable in parts; retailing your own organs is already a common way of obtaining money in less-developed countries and one which is becoming increasingly common in the industrialized world (Dalla Costa, 1996: 114).[11]

The sophistication of the ideology that underpins our present economic system lies in its ability to construct a convincing logic that *includes* the reservations and resistance of its critics, and which thereby accommodates and creates what Antonio Gramsci termed *hegemony* (1971), which we will return to in a discussion of Laclau and Mouffe (1985). He employed this construct to describe social systems in stasis, a point where all the various forces in society are brought into a coherent, functioning whole, in equilibrium. When ideology loses its power to convince, force becomes necessary. The actual seizure of power may only be momentary; it is an act that is necessary to gain power and domination. In other words, to exercise power, there must be mechanisms in place to keep it going, to keep social tensions from tearing the domination apart, and it is this interplay between power and the social that postmodernists and post-structuralists, by dismissing ideology, cannot adequately address.

On a practical level, ideology is operationalized and generalized through language. Language provides the symbols and connections by which we interpret the world, even though it does not fully encompass the consciousness and feelings that any one individual may possess. As I have indicated, language can be articulated as a political construction. "Dialects with armies" can be witnessed empirically, whether it be in the former Yugoslavians' attempts to make the Serb and Croatian languages incomprehensible to each other, Webster's attempt to create an "American" English distinguishable from British English, the resurgence of dialects and languages in resistance movements around the world, or in the development of language for theory. Language involves power – whether in the nation-state or in the academy – and the exercise of that power for political ends. In this way, the post-structuralists have it partially right: this process of symbolic activity does more than construct the *ideal* mode of domination. It actively plays a part in the construction of thought as it attempts to structure experience. The literary critic Kenneth Burke invoked "terministic screens" to refer to the way that people use language to form logic from an assortment of possibilities.[12] Signification embodies categorization and principles of inclusion and exclusion, but Burke, unlike the post-structuralists, related these structures to the interests of class positions.[13]

The ideology that rationalizes capital need not be expressed by individuals in acts that are directly related to its ultimate purpose. It can be experienced by individuals as ways to further personal goals. The ability to contribute to and reap the rewards of capitalist functioning are dependent on class position and location; the *ideal* that capital presents is to achieve those marks of success and status that define the successful individual. Ideas do not operate as contained entities any more than individuals do; their genesis is elsewhere, in the social relations of society that provide the foundation for their development.

The rationalization that capitalist ideology produces may thus be masked in forms of conscious thought and action that reinforce the goals of that ideology while appearing on the surface as resistance. Expressions of difference may turn into avenues of opportunity for new markets. Examples abound, such as the incorporation and co-opting of the "sexual revolution" of the 1960s, the marketing of mood stabilizing drugs to better adapt to the violence of capitalist labor relations, the use of songs of resistance for the selling of cars, and, yes, the development of theory that stresses the rights and uniqueness of each individual "self."[14]

## The paradox of Queer theory

Because much of Queer theory confuses personal action with structural power, it asserts the primacy of the first or individual aspect, while ignoring its determinants. On an interpersonal level, we can demand and expect to be treated as equals, capable of determining our own fate. But resistance to structural power requires the more concerted energy of collective action. To analyze aspects of interpersonal power and politics in isolation from the larger structural concerns and barriers they confront denies the agency of the individual in the social. For our purposes, sexuality and gender are "site[s] of power" (Weeks, 1985: 176), and as such they need to be situated in place and time. The movements of the 1960s and 1970s located personal decisions in the realm of the political.[15] But it is in the discussion of what *level* of politics is being brought to the forefront that Queer theory has failed to make inroads, and this has worked against this essential element of political relationships.

While certain Queer theorists celebrate difference and see the refusal to identify as a radical act (cf. esp. Butler, 1991; 1994), we can see that these assertions are supportive of the same ideal of the individual as self that capitalism has created. It attempts to take the logical effect and material consequence of the capitalist system, the reified individual, and use it to rectify inequality. Queer theory needs to account for the difference between the "self" and the "individual" in much the same way that it needs to incorporate "postmodernity" into the realm of the postmodern.

A perception that we can reject binary systems of gender without rejecting all bases for identity, however temporary they may be, is necessary for true resistance and social change. We cannot fight alone, not against a world system with military power and the ever-present threat of force and economic destruction. If "all things queer," then, is to become anything more than a novel digestion of difference, it must include the individual as more than the self as text. It must accommodate the individual in society.

## The use of the concept of culture

As I have suggested, within the academic disciplines, "culture" has become an enigma that encompasses all, from the nature of corporate and voluntary organizations to the characteristics of whole populations. In the social sciences, it has become contentious, the dividing line coming between those who see the interpretation and interaction of symbols as a unique human activity that characterizes culture (cf. Geertz, 1973) to Wolf's (1982) conclusion that the use of the concept "threatens to turn names into things" (1982: 3) or to assume "an inherent coherence over time" (1982: 388). Wolf prefers "Pierre Bourdieu's adaptation of Marcel Mauss's concept of *habitus*, to show how people acquire 'durable and transposable dispositions' through conditioning to the institutional landscape of social settings" (Bourdieu and Wacquant, 1992: 115–139; Wolf, 1999: 10).

The place of "culture" in Queer theory has also sparked debates around its usefulness, aptly summarized by Butler in answer to her critics (cf. 1998). Still, culture as a descriptor is still in popular use, and its dismissal as a category can be an over-reaction to the way in which it has been used to forgo closer analyses of the ties that bind. To use the concept of culture, then, it is necessary to define what it is and how it is being used; it can be a productive tool in delineating differences within and among communities as well as changes in belief and behavior that characterize communities and nations.

Whatever is positioned as "queer culture" bears an appropriation of a label containing an assertion of rights and recognition. The use of "culture" in this context, however, is ambiguous. It is cognized as anything not "straight," or sometimes anything that is not "gay" or "lesbian." "Culture" here, like its counterpart in most popular uses of the term, is broad enough to include anyone and any act declaring its validity and its descriptive character. Because of this generalized nature, it is necessarily vague when positioned against other aspects of a more general "culture." How does queer culture differ from that of "straight" or the "dominant" culture? What in any of these contexts does "culture" represent?

In social science, culture refers to those socially transmitted patterns of behavior characteristic of particular social groups. Individuals reconciling themselves with the larger social whole influence the way that culture is acted upon; but culture also, by definition, situates individuals. In short, culture is "that complex whole which includes knowledge, belief, art, law, customs and any other capabilities and habits acquired by members of a society," according to Edward Tyler, the nineteenth-century English scientist whose definition is most often used by social scientists. This view of culture as a descriptor of norms was modified by White (1949) to include the way in which humans harness energy in order to reproduce society.

It was a precipitous turn for cultural studies and Queer theory that Clifford Geertz (1973) redefined culture as the way in which people find meaning in their surroundings (1973: 3–32). Louise Lamphere, Helene Ragone, and Patricia Zavella note the influence of the Geertzian definition on cultural studies, remarking that

> Cultural studies scholars theorize about diasporas, emerging discourses, new cultural tropes, and the hybridized nature of identities that characterize a "postmodern" world. Even though they have adopted the language of cultural anthropology, cultural studies theorists often focus more on power through cultural representation and less on the pragmatics of power or on individual and collective responses to power.
>
> (Lampere *et al.*, 1977: 2)

Like its popular reckoning, contemporary uses of culture in academic literature are often employed without specific definition, or in terms so ordinary, as Raymond Williams (1958) puts it, that it defies specific application. This has led to the use of culture as a postmodern ambiguity, so that any definition of "culture" disappears as soon as it is noted. This use misses the significant symbolic aspects of cultural artifacts and their influence on behavior. The "all that is solid melts into air" that Marshall Berman (1982) claims is the defining characteristic of postmodern society is aptly critiqued by Willis (1993), who argues that symbolic activity has to be re-cognized in terms of the symbolic creativity in everyday life. In other words, the analyses have to catch up with the movement of the real world.[16]

The idea of culture is most often used to refer to patterns of behavior and life within a community, the regularly recurring activities of material and social arrangements. This is the sense in which culture refers to the realm of observable behavior, to things and events "out there." It is the organized system of knowledge and belief by which people structure their experience, formulate acts, and choose between alternatives.

As shared systems of meanings, culture includes codes of behavior and norms of everyday behavior that are not necessarily conscious, from driving in traffic to the knowledge of where foodstuffs are shelved in the market. But it also includes the creation and use of commodities, endowing them with social meanings that influence the way in which we define our own experience.

The acceptance of social norms through the social/common psyche, then, is due to a complex process which can be described as a dialectical relation between people and society, as they both produce and reproduce the social relations in which they are embedded. It does not assume relativity. As Williams also noted:

> A common culture is not, at any level, an equal culture ... A culture in common in our own day, will not be the simple all-in-all society of an old dream. It will be a very complex organization, requiring continual adjustment and redrawing ... we will have to insure the means of life, and the means of community. But what will then, but these means, be lived, we cannot know or say.
>
> (Williams, 1985: 304–320)

Involved in this are economic, historical, and psychical processes that determine the ideological context for political relations.

# Part II

# Evaluating practice

# 3   Considering sex, gender, and difference

Proponents of Queer theory would have it that there are as many possibilities for genders as there are those filling them. Western cultures, on the other hand, dichotomize categories of gender and sexuality into either/or patterns. We have in practice distinguished between nature and nurture, the individual and society, public versus private, and culture as against biology. It follows that heterosexuality and homosexuality have been popularly posed as binary categories of sexuality *and* gender, opposing poles that neither recognize nor acknowledge the differences between or among the two domains. In the Darwinian tradition, "male" and "female" are the elements of all biological life, or put in a familiar way, anatomy is destiny.

Discussions of sex and gender are most illustrative when backed by observable behavior. From Margaret Mead's *Sex and Temperament* (1935) and *Male and Female* (1949) to the more recent *Gender/Sexuality Reader* (edited by Roger N. Lancaster and Micaela di Leonardo, 1997), anthropologists have long advocated "participation" and "observation." Although ethnographers have their own screens through which they view data, these methods often yield a more complete modality of social inquiry about on-the-ground activity.

More recent anthropological studies of sexuality and gender have been influenced by a "practice approach" that developed during the 1970s and 1980s. During this period ethnographers, recognizing the past limitations of field studies, started to show that women, in particular, were under-represented in the anthropological literature. This realization led many to adopt the position that the ethnographer is not only an "objective observer" but is influenced by his or her own location in the social world. During the 1970s and 1980s, anthropologists and social philosophers such as Ortner (1978), Sacks (1975), and Reiter (1975), and many others, began to develop a feminist anthropology that reevaluated the place and the *situation* of women in the ethnographic context (cf. Lamphere *et al.*, 1977: 8). They recognized that, until relatively recently, anthropological fieldworkers have been overwhelmingly male, distorting the position of women in many societies. By way of illustration Evelyn Blackwood (1989) showed that although the !Kung Bushmen are among the most studied social groupings on earth, it wasn't until Shostak's

(1981) life history of a !Kung woman that it became widely known that lesbian relationships among the !Kung were common and accepted. In recent years, the position of women and men, and of sexuality and gender in general, have all been reevaluated in light of current fieldwork. The concern with the place of women and inequality had antecedents in the writings of other anthropologists, particularly Leacock (1972; 1981) and the collections represented in Leacock and Nash (1977), Etienne and Leacock (1980), Nash and Safa (1980), Nash (1970; 1978; 1979), and Safa (1981), among others. But these particular anthropologists' focus on the relations of production and the distribution of the rewards of labor identified them as "Marxists," a label that continues to make some feminists uncomfortable.[1] Like the ethnographic research in anthropology, the literature on homosexuality has been dominated by male same-sex behavior, with little consideration of lesbian and even less about transgendered behavior.

The dichotomies of biology/culture, nature/nurture, and heterosexual/ homosexual represent particular historical conditions. They are methodological viewpoints that require a closer analysis.[2] Gender assumes culture, roles, and behavior, and at least a rudimentary division of labor.[3] Much of gender theory has been, and to an extent still is, based on Freud's theories of psychosexual development, which imply that early experience "imprints" a gendered identity onto the child. Some of the early scholars of sexology recognized that the problems of certain persons were not accountable in this dualistic system, but instead of ensuring that they were investigated as a subject of analysis, they were designated unclassifiable.

Because most nineteenth- and twentieth-century writings on sex and gender roles have overplayed the role of biology, many have reacted by dismissing biology altogether as a legitimate field of inquiry. The very existence of technology that permits the changing of sex and the terms of reproduction, however, puts this trend on questionable ground.

The argument that gender, often used interchangeably with sex, is either determined by "nature" or constructed by "culture" represents a continuation of debates about human nature that include assumptions about power in Western culture. The proposition that the body's genetics determines behavior will continue until the ideologies of power that position the credibility of this argument are themselves replaced.

In his discussion of the history of sexology, Gilbert Herdt (1993) points out that homosexuality, as a designation, existed slightly before the category of heterosexuality. Deviations from the norm were first labeled "inversions" and later, with the further construction of medicine and psychiatry, "corrupt object choices." But as Pearce and Roberts (1976) show for industrializing Britain, the sexual binary has reinforced the social regulation of sexual behavior. Somerville (1997) notes how this movement in the science of sexuality also generated a basis for racism by labeling differing phenotypes as "oversexed" and "primitive":

Is it merely a historical coincidence … that the classification of bodies as either "homosexual" or "heterosexual" emerged at the same time that the United States was aggressively policing the imaginary boundary between "black" and "white" bodies? … the mutual effects of discourses on homosexuality and race remain unexplored.

(Sommerville, 1997: 38)

The differences between black and white, American and non-American (particularly African), and men and women have been essential in the rhetoric of colonial politics and in the ever-developing theories of the medical canon. The National Socialist movement in Germany, the architects of apartheid, and even the managers of multinational corporations have all used an essentialist nature of bodies and behavior as a basis for rationalizing dominant forms of managerial practices and governance.

Attempting to go beyond the hegemonic tradition of a reproductive paradigm that contains and elicits dimorphic assumptions, some cross-cultural observers of gender and sexuality have suggested that categories based on anatomical criteria are "neither universal nor valid concepts for a gendered classification system" (Herdt, 1993: 53). Sex as a reproductive act and sexual orientation are not necessarily concurrent, and gender identity and expected gender roles do not necessarily coincide. In our own culture, the descriptors of "masculine" and "feminine" are meant to be the same as gender roles, but in actuality often mask assumed orientation and sexual preference. The categories of the dominant culture may define acceptable behavior and presentation of gender and of sexual orientation, but these definitions often do not represent what is taking place in practice. Given this ambiguity, Herdt (1993) argues that the discussion in which the terms are assumed as sex is biology and gender is culture must be discontinued. He supports Kessler and McKenna's (1978) proposal that "the categories of male and female – based on anatomical criteria – are neither universal nor valid concepts for a gendered classification system" (Herdt, 1993: 53). Clarifying their position, Herdt further states that,

Instead of morphology, [Kessler and McKenna] suggest that the (North American) Berdache is "a third category, separate from male and female." Not only do "they contend that a dual gender classification system is merely a cultural construction," as Bolin has noted, but they leave aside the question of whether sexual desire or practice enters in. This is significant because, in the arena of sexuality, social pressures and power relations are never far from the expression of third sex and third gender roles.

(Herdt, 1993: 53–54)

In the literature on gender, the Hijras of India are well cited in the ongoing debates around gender and homosexuality, including the relationship of roles to behavior. Hijras speak of themselves as being holy and separate. They dress like women and often perform female mimicry. They engage in coarse and burlesque behavior, often berating people into giving them money. Many of the Hijras insist they were born that way. Emasculation by gender mutilation is a caste duty and carried out in a ritual context. Intersexuality, impotence, emasculation, and transvestitism are all part of Hijra roles and with them comes sexual abstinence, which is said to redirect energy towards otherworldliness. In practice, however, there is much tension between the real and the stated: many Hijras do practice homosexuality and prostitution, including man/boy sex. Nanda (1993) shows that, although mythology claims that Hijras practice abstinence, many join the community for the opportunity to engage in sexual relations with men while enjoying the security and safety of the group. She notes that in classical Hinduism there is a category for a third sex, itself divided into a number of categories, all of which provide for alternative types of sexual gratification. Unlike Western cultures, in which sexuality and gender are often equated, in many parts of India sexual object choice does not necessarily coincide with a publicly perceived gender role. Gender is thus not automatically perceived as connected to sexuality or sexual desire but as dependent on the cultural constructs of particular group identities.

But this is just one example. The ethnographic record is resplendent with instances of gender switching that do not match biological or desired sex and do not conform to culturally stated categories. Trumbach (1993) refers to the phenomenon of "mollies" and "tommies" or "sapphists" in eighteenth-century Europe, and goes so far as to suggest that there were clearly four genders operating in this period: male, female, mollies, and sapphists. He argues that these differences are precisely cultural in nature and are conditioned and confirmed by cultural codes and symbols. Of course, these distinctions are themselves intellectually and culturally constructed. Certainly nineteenth-century Britain did not recognize four genders. But we can see here that a classification system which places emphasis on dimorphism can be easily contested. Certainly the desire for an individual technologically to transform morphology by having a sex change to match inner feelings, deemed necessary and made possible in a specifically Western context, makes clear that more ethnographic work is needed to explore the relationship between morphology, sex, gender, and culture, and the way that individual feelings are actualized.

Despite recent trends attempting to offer a more integrated and dialectical relationship between mind/body, individual/society and culture/nature, the basic argument about essential differences, whether biologically based or culturally constructed, still remains.[4] Indeed, given this reality, methodologies shifting the emphasis from binaries to dialectical methodologies become subversive. What does it mean to acknowledge that individual needs and experiences are more complicated than our present system of governance is willing to presume and to account for? What are the implications for understanding that the norms of behavior set out by advertising machines and work-ethic spinners are themselves constructed? Why has the substantial ethnographic evidence on sexuality, multiple genders, and gender switching been, to all public intents and purposes, ignored by the culture at large, as the "gay gene" advocates demonstrate so well?

## The essentialist/constructionist debate: from troubles to difference

The essentialist/constructionist debate closely follows the tracks of the nature/nurture controversy. It has taken on a new energy as the search for the "gay gene" and lesbian "neural anomalies" generates publicity in a continuing effort to medicalize differences in gender and sexuality. The headlines emphasize sexualness rather than behavior. The embracing of the "gay gene" by many in the queer movement brings into focus the power of dominant ideology over resistance movements and the dangers of politics played for momentary gain.

The constructionist position, in contrast, emphasizes the social roles and behaviors that build the categories of normalized behavior. Many have claimed, however, that in the noble attempt to prove that we are not isolated individuals, this position glosses over the differences in and among cultural and individual experience. As Epstein tells us, "Constructionism has no theory of the intrapsy-chic; it is unable to specify the ways in which desire comes to be structured over the course of people's lives" (1987: 14).

While Epstein, for one, would claim that social analyses cannot account for the intra-psychic, anthropologists have asserted that even "the seemingly most intimate details of private existence [are] actually structured by larger social relations" (Ross and Rapp, 1997: 51). The intra-psychic, in other words, is also a social phenomenon. Biology, too, like culture, is lived and experienced and translated into symbolic and social terms. Ross and Rapp point out that in eighteenth-century Europe, for example, many of the craft associations had elaborate rituals and vows of celibacy that delayed marriage, effectively enforcing the solidarity of the group. But as industrial relations changed in Europe, so did the family. Working-class youths became freer to participate in sexual behavior, a correlate to their earlier entry into the labor force as "free" holders of labor that could be bought and sold.

There are many cultures that prohibit sexual relations until formal rites of passage have taken place, removing people from the sexual market at times when their participation could destabilize social relations. In Western terms, while sex may often seem an intensely individual matter, or at least a private one, it also has far-reaching effects for the social domains in which it operates.

In the post-structuralist world of academic queer politics, the essentialist/

constructionist debate has taken a new turn. A critique of essentialism is now put to use as a tactic against those who would emphasize alliance over difference, and identity over deconstruction. This is what Judith Butler proposes in *Gender Trouble*. Sex, gender, and desire become "compulsory orders," or categories that are packed with assumed meaning (Butler, 1990: 6). Butler replaces the term *essentialism* with *foundational*, but all the same, sexuality and gender, for Butler, are better understood as personal attributes without an identity derived from an all-encompassing category. Sexuality and gender then become, by an alternative set of rules, incomparable in and among cultures. While the attempt to dismantle essentialist/foundational concepts as mechanically constructionist building blocks is not without merit, the form that it has taken dismisses the basis for the argument without offering alternative modalities. Can we simply dismiss gender as a category? Can we dismiss categories? Butler contends that,

> If gender is the cultural meanings that the sexed body assumes, then a gender cannot be said to follow from a sex in any one way. Taken to its logical limit, the sex/gender distinction suggests a radical discontinuity between sexed bodies and culturally constructed genders ... When the constructed status of gender is theorized as radically independent of sex, gender itself becomes a free-floating artifice, with the consequence that *man* and *masculine* might just as easily signify a female body as a male one, and *woman* and *feminine* a male body as easily as a female one.
>
> (Butler, 1991: 6)

The particular construction necessarily ignores the historical specificity of cultural development. Culture is not relative, spinning into place as if by cosmic accident. A closer analysis of the context and the reproduction of culture is needed for these concepts to become intelligible.[5]

As in Herdt's (1993) discussion of third genders, Butler acknowledges trouble with current concepts of sex and gender, but unlike Herdt she then proceeds to deconstruct them as pejoratively "prediscursive" or constructed as prior to culture by the act of discourse. Her formulation rests on the same tautology that she rejects: discourse apparently produces the agency of prediscursive normality, but the discourse depends on the production of prediscursive foundations in order to substantiate its regulatory power (1991: 6–7). While she points out that gender is not infinitely variable, her argument relies on the assertion that it is *discourse* that limits the possibilities of gender within culture. Politics and difference become the variables of discourse, rather than the other way around; indeed, the economy is but a signifying realm (1991: 11).[6] This linguistic reductionism masks the complex ways that culture and society reproduce difference and the use of difference for exploitation and oppression.

Seidman takes a more tempered view in his *Difference Troubles* (1997), even as he acknowledges his debt to Butler in the title of his book.[7] Noting that difference has not been a major theme in sociological theory, he argues that including difference and subjectivity "disturbs foundational notions of the subject, knowledge, history and politics that give coherence to much social thinking" (1997: ix). In his view, "constructive political projects" must use a level of analysis that does not assume coherence. Making the point that the social sciences have only recently considered sexuality a serious topic and have not yet connected the issues of sexuality and power to hegemonic control on either the local or global levels, Seidman proceeds to make a distinction between social theory and sociological theory, proposing that the former entails the examination of current issues while the latter paints a broader canvas that looks to the underpinnings and workings of society as a whole. Thus, Marx's *The Communist Manifesto*, Weber's *The Protestant Ethic and the Spirit of Capitalism*, and Durkheim's *The Division of Labor in Society* were all written with contemporary issues of their times in mind. They confront current issues at hand and are therefore classified as social theory rather than sociological theory (Seidman, 1997: 44–45).

This arbitrary distinction between social theory and sociological theory blurs the intent of the writers as much as it constantly threatens to relegate history to the status of a footnote. Is *The Communist Manifesto* invalid because it was written in the nineteenth century? Does the date of the writing thus invalidate all of Marx's writings, whose subject was the development of capitalism? Can we assume that Weber's and Durkheim's texts hold no value beyond their concern with the German middle class and the Third Republic? Finally, do all analyses that take objective conditions as their starting point become outdated for sociological theory as soon as they are written? The intent here is not to provide a sustained critique of Seidman's work, for he has admirably raised issues that warrant consideration in the present climate of post-structuralist theory. But there is an unstated subtext here that the "social theory" of Marx, for example, has become "sociological theory" in post-World War II academic circles, and this position has wider implications for the nature of theory in general.

Let us use, for instance, modernization theory as advanced by Walter Rostow and his followers during the 1950s and 1960s, which assumed that the United States and the apparently successful economies of the western European countries had found a model of development that supported sustained development. Modernization theory was a so-called objective theory of development, given current world-wide economic conditions. It would be, then, as Seidman would have it, "social theory." The path for development of "less-advanced" countries lay in convincing them that the modernization model, outlined in his *Stages of Economic Growth* (1960), could provide for economic success. The motivation for these ideas was far from academic. Rostow's work became a manual for US policy in much of the less-developed world and was used as a blueprint for the war in

Vietnam. The US military's campaign of deforesting the countryside was built on the assumption that forcing people into cities would provide a more progressive template for the initiation of these growth opportunities, while maintaining control of divergent and resistant populations. A critical aspect of such theories was the tenet that unsuccessful attempts to promote growth were a problem of *attitude*. If economic growth failed, it was because the will of the people had been misdirected. Logically, then, this strategy could not misfire. The model provides for the failure to be "modernized" in given contexts, where inadequate leadership is blamed and where differences outweigh conformity. Thus, the failure of US policy in Vietnam could be explained by attributing to the Vietnamese a resistance to correct economic policies, coupled with an unwillingness on the part of the American people to sustain military action. The theory itself, both universalizing and total, is infallible.

While certainly centered on then-contemporary issues, modernization theory is still invoked to explain the failure of less capital-intensive economies. Far from simply being "social theory," as explanation, it has had significant sociological consequences, as have the classic works of Marx, Weber, and Durkheim. The arbitrary distinction blurs the development of theory and its consequences.

Responding to a critique of his "The End of Sociological Theory,"[8] Seidman states that his writing does not constitute a critique of contemporary society. In his words, "nowhere do I connect my critique of sociological theory to a substantive view of contemporary America or 'the Modern West' " (1997: 203). He is, rather,

> sympathetic with Rorty's affirmation of contemporary Western societies while pushing his liberalism in a decidedly stronger pluralistic and demo-cratic direction. "Democratic pluralism," roughly speaking, is the standpoint of the later work of Foucault (1980) and Lyotard (1984) as well as that of many postmodernists, feminists and queer theorists. For my part, I do not see postmodernism as entailing a complete break from contemporary West-ern modernity ... American postmodernists generally stand opposed to those left critiques that reduce modernity to instrumental reason, technoc-racy, or capitalist domination.
>
> (1997: 204)

The application of Rostow's theory to US policy in Vietnam provides an example of the indissolubility of social and sociological theory. The US involvement in Vietnam was as much a result of the workings of capitalism, the broader picture, as it was of the issue of Vietnamese resistance to colonial policy (the current issue at the time). As a result of the implementation of Rostow's modernization theory through military and economic policy throughout the world, governments, peoples, and economies have been ravaged in an attempt to make them conform to the needs of capitalist accumulation. That the real motivation was profit was never mentioned.

## Queer and different

The place of queer peoples is connected to the place of other oppressed minorities and to the West's history of domination and colonial policies, as any of the writers under discussion would readily acknowledge. The extent to which similarities of circumstances exist, however, is often glossed over in the debates dominating the definition and significance of difference. The history of domination has shaped the way gender is defined, as well as the way famines are organized, economic disasters broadcast, and the division of labor segmented.

While Seidman is correct in asserting that, indeed, postmodernist thought does not break with the contemporary Western traditions, what of political economy? By accepting the validity of Western organization, and therefore capitalist relations of production, Seidman here compartmentalizes the relations of production as a separate sphere from interpersonal relations. The placement of the individual in subjectivity is countermanded in the analyses of radical economists such as Mandel (1972), and the primarily sociological writers such as Harvey (1989), and the literary critic Eagleton (1986; 1997).[9]

Gender is a divisive force within gay politics, splitting groups into male and female, bisexual and queer. Like the past movements that Queer theory eschews, each constituent meta-identity protests that their specific interests have not been adequately recognized. A more comprehensive view acknowledges that these divisions reproduce the tensions within the larger society and beyond queer communities; these questions of power, gender, race, and class are imbedded in the workings of present-day society. That they should also prove divisive within queer communities attests to the interconnection of "queer" with the larger culture and its effects on the trajectories of daily life. Lesbians, transsexuals, bisexuals, and racial "others" *have* been silenced within the gay and lesbian movement in the same way that women, queers, and non-white peoples have been silenced and oppressed in Western culture. Yet instead of recognizing that the differences have to do with the similarities of subjugation, Queer theory has led a shift toward issues of subjectivity, both within and among peoples. Why is this?

The anthropologist Allen Young argues that "Because I am a white male homosexual, a New Yorker, a leftist, most of what I say is from that perspective. There are other homosexuals – Third World Peoples, lesbians, transvestites – about whom I can say little. They speak for themselves" (in Seidman, 1997: 119). As a Queer theorist, Young does not pretend to reflect the experience of LGBT peoples within the dominant culture, or describe their interdependence with and existence within capitalist relations. It would seem to be an extreme reaction to "totalizing" descriptions of experience.

But such refutations of observable experience take on meaning in the lives of populations that have seen their history written by others and their lives dictated from the outside. Those from neocolonial states have insisted that they assume responsibility for rewriting their representational literature as an act of leadership. The refusal to recognize possible alliances with those subjugated within the same social context, on the other hand, is an act of negation – a *lack* of understanding that leadership comes from identifications rooted in the same struggle. Rather than discover the similarities that subtend gender, race, and class, those who would disavow the ability to speak with and about others disclaim the existence of any real coalition. Such a strategy is not only disastrous for the future, it also ignores the past. In Lancaster and Di Leonardo's words,

> the black civil rights movement, associated with other American race-minority struggles and with the florescence of international antiracist (building on earlier anticolonial) movements, spurred recognition of the ways in which sexuality and the very perception of human corporeality are not only "gendered" and understood in terms of "appropriate" or "normal" desires but are also intimately and intricately inscribed with race. In popular culture, this insight heightened awareness that "the personal is political," and that sexuality and power are mutually imbricated. At the academic and intellectual levels, this insight drew on and helped to further earlier work investigating the intersections of class, caste, and sexuality.[10]
>
> (Lancaster and Di Leonardo, 1997: 3)

At the other end of the spectrum we have the historian Joan Scott, who, in her "The Evidence of Experience" (1993), makes the simple point that many have been stressing since the reevaluation of scholarship in the 1960s: description is influenced by the writer's point of view, or what Patricia Williams, following Gayatri Spivak (1987), calls "subject-position." Spivak means the position in which one is made subject; Williams refers to the social position in which the writer finds oneself (Williams, 1991: 134). Instead of remarking that the author's position needs to be clear, however, Scott uses the forum to deconstruct the work of those who use political economy to help explain social change.[11] Her own motive for her adamant attack on the historian E.P. Thompson's seminal *The Making of the English Working Class* (1980) is telling, if not clearly stated, as she asserts that he essentializes class and thus "naturalizes" the differences among individuals (that her position therefore ahistorically "naturalizes" capitalism is not part of her analysis). In a strange project, Scott too implies that language is more important than agency, thought more important than action. Ultimately she attempts to discredit the relations of production through her insistence on the primacy of "experience":

[E.P. Thompson's] use of it, experience, because it is ultimately shaped by relations of production, is a unifying phenomenon overriding other kinds of diversity. Since these relations of production are common to workers of different ethnicities, religions, and trades they necessarily provide a common denominator and emerge as a more salient determinant of "experience" than anything else. In Thompson's use of the term experience is the start of a process that culminates in the realization and articulation of social conscious-ness, in this case a common identity of class. It serves as an integrating func-tion, joining the individual to the structural and bringing together diverse people into that coherent (totalizing) whole which is distinctive of a class.

(Scott, 1993: 404)

Scott maintains that "In Thompson's account class is finally an identity rooted in structural relations that preexist politics" (1993: 405). But, in fact, Thompson never does this: politics and class are inseparable, for the very basis of class is politics and domination, and both are always constructed historically.[12]

Yet Scott continues that "This kind of use of experience has the same founda-tional status if we substitute 'women's' or 'Black' or 'lesbian' or 'homosexual' [for class]" (1993: 405), leaving the reader to wonder not only why alliances are formed but why these categories exist in the first place. Are they not historically located descriptions? Do they not represent *real* conditions of oppressive action? Furthermore, what of her own location? Contradicting her own allegation, she does not refer to her place of privilege in a secured position at the Institute for Advanced Study at Princeton, an Ivy League institution well suited to reproduce the class structure of American society. Indeed, the objection to the use of "class" or "lesbian" or "homosexual" immediately has an effect that is not just disorienting but disillusioning. How would, cast in these terms, a labor leader feel about such a dismissal from his or her position? How would "homosexuals" fighting for rights within society react to her claim that the label is totalizing?[13]

Individuals may be holders of experience, but it is the culture that feeds them. Put another way, claiming that categories, labels, and identities are restrictive has the same social effect as arguments against affirmative action which claim that all categories should be eliminated. But we can see, on the ground, what effect the anti-affirmative action movement has had on education and employment. Shall we include gender and sexuality as equally attackable categories? Affirmative action recognizes that there are socially constructed categories demanding recognition *and* action. Scott's methodology does not.

If Scott's approach is anti-political, it is part of the elitist postmodern posi-tioning that we have already mentioned and which will be discussed in more detail in Chapter 5. For those of us who believe that alliances are necessary, identity is based on a commonality of experience. "Class" and "lesbian" and "homosexual" are categories of analysis precisely because they refer to the positioning of people in relation to others. The use of political economy is part of the identification of positions, as William Roseberry explains:

> the attempt to constantly place culture in time, to see a constant interplay between experience and meaning in a context in which both experience and meaning are shaped by inequality and domination is the attempt to understand the emergence of particular peoples at the conjunction of local and global histories, to place local populations in the larger currents of world history.
>
> (in Lancaster and Di Leonardo, 1997: 4)

Scott's temptation to abandon the notion of experience altogether, "given its usage to essentialize, identify and reify the subject" (1993: 412), leads us to ask: where does this leave resistance?[14] In the context of social change, is it productive to reify categories and then dismiss them, because of the danger of their "essentializing nature"? Or is it more appropriate to locate this discussion, in the true sense of the word, in a realm that acknowledges power and domination as determinant subjects in themselves? By insisting only on the relevance of position, she dismisses it, unwittingly feeding the machines of ideological production: it is hard not to conclude that despite her own desires for a more egalitarian society, it is the limits of her own positioning that is in need of inquiry.

## Solidarity and solitary analyses

Scott's focus on personal experience again raises the issue of the long-debated relationship between consciousness and social action. Political economists do not contest the social certainty that individuals experience the social as individuals, integrating the nexus of relationships that make up the whole. Still, there are similarities in the stimuli that we confront and experience as socialized beings. The "I" that many postmodernists employ disavows the validity of the social, necessarily disrupting the alliances that can lead to organizing change.

Few would contest that a psychic level of analysis is indeed necessary if we are to understand the social whole. To accomplish this, Jeffrey Weeks (1985) offers the compelling argument that we should not dismiss Freud's writings on the unconscious, particularly as they relate to "the way ... psychic reality [is] fundamentally different from biological and social reality" (1985: 129). He argues that the general dismissal of Freud for individual and social analyses has been done in the name of some of his more insignificant arguments, and Weeks argues, following Freud, that the unconscious is not a container of

> repressed instinct but ideas ... attached to drives which seek to discharge their energy, wishful impulses which are denied access to consciousness ... what fundamentally constitutes the unconscious are those wishes which are

repressed in the face of the demands of reality and in particular the repressed (and incestuous) desires of infancy: "what is unconscious in mental life is also what is infantile."

(Weeks, 1985: 129)

Weeks sees the position of the ego as part of Freud's own "Copernican revolution," "with the demonstration that the ego was not even the master in its own domain, but the subject of unconscious urges and impulses over which it has little or no initial control." Culture mediates these impulses, and identity is an achievement that is constantly undermined by the unconscious. The "repression" that becomes part of the individual becoming part of humanity is not "an imposition on our humanity but an essential stage of its emergence" (1985: 130). Thus,

> The first moment when a child realizes (or imagines) the distinction between its own body and the outside, the "other", is simultaneously the moment which announces the permanent alienation at the heart of identification ... For Freud, to be human is to be divided.
>
> (1985: 130–131)

Culture, then, always integrates the individual, as the individual integrates culture into the psyche. If there is a fundamental drive to use our energies to actualize ourselves, then in that effort of actualization it is necessary to identify with others striving to do the same. But the integration of the individual psyche into society, beliefs, and customs does not oppose the process of *individuation*, and is in fact quite central to it. The ego can still function individually, with "fixed points" as Brennan has it, depending "on its identification with others, and ideas, to maintain a sense of its individual distinctiveness, or identity" (Brennan, 1993: xii). Psychical energy is then directed at the search for identification with others, while maintaining the cohesiveness of the self. It is also the basis for becoming a full member of society.

The problem presented by the analyses of Scott, Butler, and other postmodern and post-structuralist writers influential in Queer theory is that we are left presupposing that our own psychical needs are more important than those of others and that our differences therefore hold priority over our similarities. This is what produces symbolic violence and prejudice, and unwillingness to work actively for the reconciliation of variance.

But most of all, we need to put into consideration the fact of "the reality" of our situation.[15] The Cartesian notion that "reality" can be derived from one's own experience has pitted the mind, or the psyche, against culture and, in turn, philosophy against anthropology.[16] The modern "subjectivists" of Queer theory ignore the level of analysis on which politics operates. The project is not to concentrate on the invalidity of description or experience, for the use of experience as subject, as Eagleton (1997) notes, can also be dogma. The project is rather to work in *the context* of change, recognizing differences but also stressing the importance of contextual similarities. Oscar Lewis's (1963) infamous suggestion that the problems of poverty might only be solved through individual psychoanalysis, gives a concrete example of the dilemma that exists. Imaginatively, this strategy could work, but certainly not within the framework in which we all live.

Anthropology, as the social science discipline pre-eminently concerned with the illustration of similarity and difference, has repeatedly come up against the problem of reconciling the description of what the ethnographer sees with what is being considered by the subject. This distinction is referred to by Marvin Harris (1968) as the split between the "emic" and the "etic." "Etic" refers to observable behavior; what is witnessed and can be recorded. The "emic," by contrast, refers to what "goes on" in people's heads, what emotions and thinking are actually made of. Harris concludes that the emic is an impossible field of study. But this is an overreaction. Ethnographers in the field confront this problem on a day-to-day basis, trying to distinguish and delineate between the differences among what they understand intuitively as members of their own culture, what information the "culture" under study is telling them, and what is actually occurring. Even in our own society we cannot assume that our understandings are the same as other segments of the population.

The task is therefore not to dismiss all attempts at understanding differences, but to put them in perspective. For the anthropologist Ward Goodenough, it means describing the differences among cultures:

> We start armed with the concepts our own culture has given us. We discover that we don't make distinctions that other cultures make and that we make distinctions that they don't make. To describe theirs and compare them with ours we have to find a set of concepts capable of describing their distinctions as well as our own. To do this, we have to analyze the phenomena more finely than we had to before, discovering and sorting our variables of which we were previously unaware.
>
> (Goodenough, 1970: 146)

Emic analyses provide the possibility for making comparisons, identifying similarities, and describing on-the-ground locations, and, as Nash (1981) comments, it is much like the methodology of linguists when trying to note the speech sounds of other languages. Goodenough elaborates the explanatory power of the emic/etic distinction by noting that,

> As a kind of typology, a systematic set of etic concepts is a tool for describing and comparing cultural forms ... Such etic concepts satisfy the criteria for a

comparative study of cultural forms free of ethnographic or specific cultural bias ... If they succeed in embracing all of the distinctive features needed to describe the elementary emic units of any culture, they constitute the minimum number of concepts needed to determine the universal attributes of culture and by inference from them, the universal attributes of men as creators and users of culture.

(Goodenough, 1970: 147)

To the extent that we have the capacity for empathy, we should be able to extrapolate at least some of the emotions of others in relation to our own. The danger, of course, is the projection of our own emotions onto others that produces an emotional isomorphism that makes this methodology a dangerous means on which to rely solely. For integral to the debates about the individual and society are inquiries concerning the development of consciousness and whether an individual consciousness can effectively act on society. Consciousness has its own set of determinants, including that of what is being experienced in the felt world, the energy that is directed at the individual and which the individual takes on and transforms. The standard inquiry about the direction of change – whether social action changes society or consciousness works to enact change – is yet another dualism that requires integration.

Consciousness takes many forms. Leon Trotsky (1973), while examining the problems facing the Russian Revolution, explored ways in which common experiences, including language usage, relations of work, sexism, alcohol use, and religion, all play a part in the way that members of a society think and act, and derive their consciousness, and, in turn, the effect of that consciousness on social change. Both Lenin and Trotsky were constantly aware of the changes in social stature that all members of a society, which had just gone through a significant and traumatic change, were experiencing; they were also aware of the dangers of the styles of thought that produced inequality or negatively impacted on mutual respect. In short, it was their belief that *action* precipitated change, and that consciousness could not transform on its own without an awareness of the symbolic power of the social relations of everyday activity.

Is this still relevant? Is it simply Seidman's concept of "social theory"? The mere mention of Lenin and Trotsky conjures up diabolical schemes of coercive state-induced conformity that sends shivers down the spines of many liberally-minded theorists. It has been assumed much too quickly that the "meta-narrative" of Marxism leads to Stalinism, so quickly that we are no longer obliged to read the work of Marxists, often critical, even those who were part of the left opposition during the Russian Revolution. Even Lenin himself thought that "organization" could be overdone (Lenin, 1993). But, as in the case of Freud, much of this writing, when carefully read, can be seen to have been misinterpreted and misapplied, particularly in and through the current wave of anti-

Marxism that has penetrated the queer movement. If we respect the view that the personal is political, we will see that the actions and concerns of everyday life affect the way in which we consider change. But the personal, thought of as purely psychical, is not enough, for it relies on that division of the ego that magnifies individual difference into – to use the language of psychology again – neuroses.

The dialectical interaction stressed by Lenin and Trotsky is similar to the one employed by psychoanalysts on the psychic level; it has long been realized that we cannot change our feelings and our emotions without a change in our actions. While these levels must be separately analyzed, they also have to be integrated on the cultural level. The ambivalence that we experience towards identity, towards categorization, is also psychical. An inability to form social bonds through identification, and to change them as we do, seems to be, as Weeks points out, "the negation of choice," for "identities and categorizations are also points of comfort, security and assuredness" (1985: 189). These social bonds allow for what Weeks calls "sexual communities," where "individual feelings become meaningful, and 'identity' possible" (1985: 189).

# 4 Capitalism and its transgressors

Capitalism creates divisions. The individual is separated from the group *in fact*: not only is labor power embodied in individuals as commodities bought and sold to produce profit, but capitalism is threatened by collectivities for the very reason that groups and communities form the basis for resistance to the unequal distribution of the rewards of labour. The task of those controlling capitalist interests is thus to disentangle such units into their constituent individual parts. The defining component of class struggle under capitalism has been the creation and destruction of communities and the control over the labor they can represent. The separation of the individual from society serves the attempt further to divide individuals from each other.[1]

Yet as we have discussed, during the 1970s and 1980s members of the feminist, gay, lesbian, and queer communities began to express doubt that Marxist writing and practice could adequately address their experiences. Was this phenomenon due to the writings of Marx himself, or to crudely interpreted understandings of Marx? The objection to Marxism, for many postmodernist and post-structuralist writers, has provoked a bitter backlash against Marxism as a mode of analysis and as a basis for political programs. The vehemence expressed suggests that more is at work here than a simple challenge to what has been judged as outdated theory.

Whatever the geneses, even critiques of capitalism have become passé. Marxism has been discharged in whole, often by those who have not engaged Marxist scholarship in debate.

I will explore here the implications of this shift away from Marxism for social theory and social movements. Much of the theory that claims postmodernism and post-structuralism as its forebears has substantively dismissed phenomena that create the basis for gender inequality and the divisions of identity we encounter today. To understand gender inequality, gender division, and, indeed, inequality in general, it is necessary to explore modes of reproduction that appear to us as a given, but are in fact particular historical facts.

## Capitalism, community, and identity

D'Emilio (1997), Pearce and Roberts (1976), Weeks (1985), and Greenberg and Bystryn (1996), all trace the social construction of sexual behavior, gender, and identity to the development of capitalism and the social consequences of changes in the organization of production. The naming of the homosexual in the nineteenth century was a political act. Homosexuals, argues D'Emilio, are not a "natural" group:

> Instead, they are a product of history, and have come into existence in a specific era. Their emergence is associated with the relations of capitalism; it has been the historical development of capitalism ... more specifically, its free labor system ... that has allowed large numbers of men and women in the late twentieth century to call themselves gay, to see themselves as part of a community of similar men and women, and or organize politically on the basis of that identity.
>
> (D'Emilio, 1997: 170)

Changes in the social organization of production and reproduction have necessarily included changes in the relationships among sexes, genders, families, and communities. Women, and, by extension, queers and other minorities, have been left out of the "central core" of social analysis, which has led to continuing distortions about their roles in, and integration with, society (Leacock, 1981: 13).

Queer identities are therefore closely tied to the development of capitalism. Wage labor, as part of the development of a competitive capitalism, became predominant during the nineteenth century, and with it came a freedom from the burdens of household economies where families principally functioned as units of production. In this process, families became centers of "personal life" and of consumption, and were effectively disconnected from processes of the growing phenomenon of wage labor. D'Emilio notes that the Puritans, for example, did not specifically condemn same-sex relationships; they merely prohibited *all* sexual acts outside marriage. The American colonists had no categories to describe gay or lesbian people. Like the trade associations in the nineteenth century that enacted ritualized ceremonies to discourage marriage when it would disrupt social relations, colonial Massachusetts enacted laws that prohibited unmarried individuals from living outside the family structure (Oaks in D'Emilio, 1997: 172). In an economy where children were necessary to accomplish household production, the threat posed by relationships that might challenge the stability of the family rendered extra-marital relationships unconscionable, since they had the potential fundamentally to undermine the ability of families to sustain themselves.

Likewise, responding to the necessity for family production, Christianity in Britain also condemned procreation outside marriage. As the basis for household production broke down, however, this necessity became less urgent and with it came a separation of sexuality from procreation.[2] But not entirely. It was no longer necessary for families to act as the sole socializers of free wage labor, nor was it necessary for families to be a significant basis for individual identity. But the family continued to represent stability, while the freedom of individuals to pursue sexual desire outside heterosexuality could lead, it was reasoned, to deviant forms of labor participation. Homosexuality, prostitution, and even masturbation came into popular lore as working against the family and against the state.

It is in the breakdown of family production that comes with the predominance of wage labor that we can find the bases for the anxiety and fear that come from a lessening of securely connected social bonds, not only in family life but also in communities. The medicalization of sexuality, the emergence of a "sexology," and the diagnosis of homosexuality as deviant behavior are related outcomes of these changes that have significantly transformed the basis for social life.

## The transformation of the social sphere

The changes in productive relations that occurred with the rise of competitive capitalism and industrialization transformed the social sphere in every area. Not only was the family no longer essential as a productive unit, but the expansion of capital, both locally and globally through colonial subjugation, opened up new fields of inquiry that rationalized the dominance of nation-states over others.

Medicalization, as Foucault notes, is also a relationship of domination, a way of positioning difference as abnormal, through the creation of an "ordered system of knowledge" (1990: 69). With medicalization came definitions of racial categorization. Sexism and racism developed in tandem, allowing the managers of colonialism to rationalize the difficulty of rule with reports of, for example, "oversexed females with protruding buttocks" (in Sommerville, 1997).[3] In this same period, eugenics was becoming the science of the day; race and intelligence were becoming known primarily in the arenas of evolution and genetics rather than through analyses of social systems. But sexual freedom was still a threat to the development of competitive capitalism, for wage laborers still needed to be reproduced. Thus, the spending of semen for reasons other than procreation has been, since early industrialization, synonymous with moral failure, draining the energy needed for work. In the nineteenth and early twentieth centuries it was a common explanation for why businesses failed, and why immigrants were unable to adapt to "modern" working conditions. The individual became the center of attention, moral character a primary goal.

By way of an example, Britain enacted a law in 1842 prohibiting women and young children from working in the mines. Women became popularly distinguished in two opposable classes: those who were respectable and stayed in the home, and the animalistic lower-class women who could be used by men to satisfy their lust while preserving the sanctity of marriage, or while waiting to accumulate enough wealth to produce a proper marriage (Pearce and Roberts, 1976: 58). There was a direct connection between capitalism and sexual energy during this era, as aptly expressed by a factory worker:

> The more energy you draw from a machine, the less there is left: you must not overload it. The more money you draw from a bank or a firm, the less there is left: it must not overspend. Therefore, the more a man fucks, the weaker he gets.[4]

> (Young in Pearce and Roberts, 1976: 59)

This logic still exists in popular culture, in the folklore that sex before a sports game hinders performance in the same way that money should not be carelessly "spent." The primacy of the relationship between man and machine replaced family relationships.

During the same period, the homosexual person, as medically labeled, replaced the homosexual act as the focus of inquiry and definition. It provided a basis for a growing competitive capitalism that was increasingly diversifying the division of labor.

Capitalism precipitated a change in the division of labor by moving men out of the household to sell their labor as a commodity. While traditional family relationships were transformed, the family was still essential for maintaining the healthy emotional ties that produced socialized labor. Puritan morality itself arose as new labor systems needed the family for both the discipline it fostered and the emotional cushioning it offered: women reproduced children and repaired the damage of alienated labor.

This scenario has been repeated in many forms to the present day, the family structure of the 1950s reflected in an ideal of capitalism brought home through the media and educational institutions. The turbulence of the 1960s was also part and parcel of the changes in capitalist relations of accumulation around the world that no longer sustained previous family and community relationships. As we shall see, these changes are tied to the position of the individual, the family, and beliefs about the person and institutions in society.

## The destruction of community

As capitalism has rapidly developed, the need for the family as a basis for socialized labor has lessened, and with it the need for communities to sustain them. The state has replaced the family and the community as the socializer of individuals and the enforcer of social control. In contrast to the needs of capitalist relations, however, communities have not willingly disappeared, but have emerged as sites of resistance to their destruction. In more recent times, multinational corporations have responded to the ability of communities to resist outside domination by actively fighting their influence on social life, and indeed, their very existence. In the face of resistance, corporations freely move their work sites to other areas where communities and unions are less organized. In particular, the movement of corporations offshore serves to provide, at least initially, resistance-free worksites. In the 1970s, the mass movement of factories around the world to areas where communities did not exist forced wage-seekers to travel to the worksite. This was a calculated strategy to counter incipient organization.

This separation of worker from both product and community affects every aspect of daily living and emotional life. But there *is* resistance in the ties of community to the attempt to destroy identifications on the part of outside forces. *Geographic* communities can even act as barricades against the attempt to enforce hegemony. *Emotional* communities, whether they be produced by similarities based on sex, gender, race, or class, act as centers of identification, spaces where individuals realize that there are others like themselves and which provide a counter to the alienation caused by rejection and discrimination. Communities provide alternatives to the goals of capitalist production. But there have also been successful attempts at the destruction of communities that have produced tragic results. María Dalla Costa notes the extreme cases of individual or group decisions to commit suicide because the basis for survival has been destroyed:

> It is significant, that, according to Italian Press reports in 1993–94, many cases of suicide in Italy are due to unemployment or to the fact that the only work available is to join a criminal gang. While, in India, the "tribal people" in the Narmada valley have declared a readiness to die by drowning if work continues on a dam which will destroy their habitat and, hence, their basis for survival and cultural identity.
>
> (Dalla Costa, 1996: 113)

## Communities in late capitalism

With the spread of transnational companies and corporations without borders, we have reached a new stage of attempted hegemonic control. The shift from the extraction of goods and services by the advanced capitalist countries from "other" economies to a concentration on the usurpation of energy in both nature and labor in those countries has transformed the relationships among populations and within communities world-wide. The speed-up of production, the forced migration of individuals and families for work, and the continuing destruction of natural resources all have a profound effect on the access to resources which make self-realization possible. Women and the lower-paid segments of the labor force are the primary targets of transnational corporations seeking the lowest labor costs. This current expansion is strikingly similar, particularly with regard to the position of women and minorities, to that which took place in the industrializa-tion of America and Europe during the nineteenth century (Nash and Fernández-Kelley, 1983: xi). At the same time, there is increasing poverty as the forces of capitalist production separate people from their land and from their basis for subsistence agriculture.

These "advances" by capitalism have radically transformed cultures on many levels. The use of the family as a means of social control has increasingly lessened as labor becomes more individualized, more de-skilled, and thus more expend-able around the world. But the consequences of such shifts can also be devastating. The spread of AIDS in East Africa, by men forced to travel to earn wages, is but one example of a freedom of behavior that does not necessarily reflect healthy self-expression.

The consequences of these changes in the advanced capitalist countries have also been profound. With industry seeking cheaper labor elsewhere, the preponderance of lower-paid service employment, or the loss of employment altogether, has become commonplace. Despite statistics in the US showing record levels of employment and an economy that is breaking profit records, what is not reported are the locations of this profit or the continued lowering of the standard of living that for many exists alongside the apparent good news.

Capitalism, as a mode of labor organization, is now rarely used as a conceptual tool to analyze the accumulation of profit and the consequent injustices that are created. "The Market," as Miller (1997) notes, is now more often invoked than "capitalism" to dramatize the "naturalness" of capitalist relations.

What does this mean for sexuality and gender? Changes in lifestyles and in the organization of communities are always accompanied by transformations in gender relations and in the expression of sexuality. Women and men, when separated from their communities, may be more free to exhibit sexual desire and behavior that might not have been condoned or even possible in a structurally stable community. The ideology that rationalizes inequalities on a global scale also affects self-expression and moral codes governing behavior in every context. With the advancing alienation of workers from communities, there arises the primacy of the individual as a responsible agent. Both gradually and suddenly, individuals are increasingly in charge of their own fates. We are reproached for our failure to eke out a living, while celebrated for taking charge. As I have noted, this ideology, and the *ideal that accompanies it*, have contradictory consequences. The failure of most to achieve a comfortable lifestyle generates a need to apportion blame. Particularly in the advanced capitalist countries with long histories of rationalized economies, this blame is typically both focused on oneself and on other individuals or groups. It is rarely directed at corporations with bureaucratic structures that allow for distance from individual concerns. A self-involvement unknown in pre-capitalist societies thus promotes the social and individual dis-ease that characterizes modern society.

Late capitalism is justified by calculation and statistical means. Welfare roles must be cut, trade simplified and enhanced, environmental programs eased, and social programs eliminated to remain "competitive." While the destruction of education, health programs, and other social services are lamented, these actions become rationalized as necessary evils to further *our* goal of success. In reality, of course, the object is the goal of increased profit.

The increased alienation of individuals from communities is reflected in social theory. Because these developments appear as *natural*, and because much of academic theory mirrors as well as reinforces the society at large, it has become commonplace to assume that concepts that promote the further individuation of the individual are the correct direction for academic development. While critiquing the tendency of Marxists and political economists to "naturalize" the categories of class, race, and gender relations, Queer theorists have mistaken the "naturalizing" tendencies that rationalize capitalist accumulation with modes of analysis, such as political economy, that can provide the basis for the development of alternative explanations. The result is that the subtext of increased alienation and inequality is ignored.

Jameson (1991) argues that the concept of alienation in late capitalism has been replaced with fragmentation (1991: 14). Fragmentation highlights the increased separation of people from one another that is now taking place. It is located in a generalized and growing lack of cultural affect that distinguishes our present period from our past. Which is not to say, in Jameson's words, that "the cultural products of the postmodern era are utterly devoid of feeling, but rather that such feelings – which it may be better and more accurate, following J.-F. Lyotard, to call 'intensities' – are particularly now free floating and impersonal" (1991: 16). Here, many postmodernists and post-structuralists argue, is the disappearance of the individual as object, where people exist as an abstraction rather than on the ground.[5] Yet what is really completed with this disappearance is the *objectification* of the individual, alone and incomparable. The *idea* of difference becomes embedded in culture:

> What we must now ask ourselves is whether it is not precisely this semi-autonomy of the cultural sphere that has been destroyed by the logic of late capitalism. Yet to argue that culture is today no longer endowed with the relative autonomy it once enjoyed as one level among others in earlier moments of capitalism (let alone in precapitalist societies) is not necessarily to imply its disappearance or extinction. Quite the contrary; we must go on to affirm that the dissolution of an autonomous sphere of culture throughout the social realm, to the point at which everything in our social life – from economic value and state power to practices and to the very structure of the psyche itself – can be said to have become "cultural" in some original and yet untheorized sense. This proposition is, however, substantially quite consistent

with the previous diagnosis of a society of the image or simulacrum and a transformation of the "real" into so many pseudoevents.

(Jameson, 1991: 48)

The fragmentation of social life repeats itself in the idea that sexuality and gender are separate and autonomous from bureaucratic state organization. If, as in Jameson's terms, differences can be *equated*, then this should not pose a problem for the generation of resistance to inequality. If, however, as is more often accomplished in postmodern and post-structuralist writings, this evolves into a theoretical presumption that makes that equation impossible, then the dominant modes of power will prevail without opposition. The danger, of course, is that while we concentrate on decentering equation and identity, we succeed in promoting the very goals of global capitalism that work against the formation of communities or provide the means to destroy those that already exist, and with them, any hope for political action. The struggle to form, maintain, or prevent the destruction of community in late capitalism, then, is perhaps the most challenging quest of our times.

For those of us who are not included in traditional sources of community building – in particular, the families in which we were raised – the building of an "affectional community ... must be as much a part of our political movement as are campaigns for civil rights" (Weeks, 1985: 176). This building of communities requires identification with others. If we cannot recognize traits that form the bases of our identification with others, how then can communities be built? The preoccupation of Foucault, as one example, with the overwhelming power of "master narratives," breeds a resignation where emphasis is placed on individual resistance that, ironically, ends up reinforcing the "narrative" itself.

Resistance to capitalism, then, involves practical struggle on issues that affect all of us on an everyday basis. We cannot pretend to disengage from the reality of discrimination or oppression and claim that we are fulfilling a task of resistance by refusing to engage the domination that exists.[6]

## Politics and lifestyle

From the quiet but contentious beginnings over open recognition and participation that characterized the early homophile movements, to the radical restructuring of strategy and theory that came with the movements of the 1960s and 1970s, and to the more mainstream tendencies of the current period, the nature of "political" in Queer movements remains in flux.

In line with the popular culture of the current era, the political is often correlated with "lifestyle." Bemoaning the difficulty of maintaining the energy that produces action, many have chosen to assert their independence from past left-wing tactics. The shift has been toward working for a full integration of rights (illustrated by the fights for the right to marry and for the right to fight in the military), or to adopting lifestyles that proclaim the similarities between queer and "straight" modes of living, and/or to the third alternative: the proclamation of "queer" as a fact, a mode of self-consciousness that recognizes and embraces difference without necessarily defending it through action.

The popularity of Queer theory suggests that the third option is, for the moment, very much in evidence in university settings. The fights for the right to participate in components of the dominant culture correspond closely to the general neo-conservatism that we are now witnessing. The radical action that was prompted by the recognition that AIDS was a disease that gained pandemic status from lack of attention is now being superceded by a belief that the proper integration of queers will have the power to change and prevent overt discrimination. Moreover, if we simply refuse to engage the actors of domination, as Queer theory suggests, then the problems will in any case become moot. But how might such integration occur, and is it possible with our present understandings of the political process?

If we recognize that the oppression of queer peoples is part of a larger exploitation of human beings, which includes modes of colonialism and xenophobia, can we consistently believe that participation in the very military, for example, that enforces this oppression is an objectively reasonable goal? If we recognize that marriage is primarily a failed institution in the culture at large, which focuses the energy of individuals on an unachievable ideal, can we comfortably claim that this is a progressive goal of social change? Does it make sense, in the face of these circumstances, to disengage?

## Consuming desire

> and we are calling our cover star, John Bartlett, an American Hero – yes, we believe that fashion designers can indeed be heroes …
>
> (Editorial, *Out Magazine*, July 1998)

> The Great Gay (Shopping) List *is* the "gay community."
>
> (Simpson, 1996)

Capitalism also "naturalizes" consumption. It creates an ideal of "having" that is easily projected to demarcate correct appearance and behavior, and which is enforced by marketing tools. Consumption is part of the circulation of capital that sustains production and the surplus value that creates accumulation and wealth. Driven to the fringe by homophobia and discrimination, queer communities have fought for acceptance through both celebrating that fringe and by fighting to become part of the mainstream. By "mainstreaming" I mean the acceptance of the norms of the politics of the dominant culture and of consumption in an effort to travel the path to a higher social status. Whether the focus is on a politics that urges the acceptance of queers on the same basis as the heterosexual norm – such as marriage or the right to be in the military – or on the accumulation of *things* that symbolize normality, queer communities often seem to be responding to a strong social pressure to conform. Even the *fringe* has a certain cachet in capitalism, in the terms of counter-cultural production and consumption. It is in itself a market.

To one extent or another, we all wear uniforms. This form of expression is grounded in a need for acceptance, for self-affirmation and for identity. What we wear and what we own is a reflection of our perceived status.

The popular literature on queer lifestyles is overwhelmingly directed at gay, white, primarily privileged males. That this should be so is not an enigma: it reflects the values of the larger society in which we all live, and it is no surprise that these values are reflected in the literature of queer popular culture.

The mainstreaming of queer politics is proceeding assertively. We are becoming used to seeing images of "normal" gay couples, such as the stereotypes of gay lifestyles that are regularly displayed on TV sitcoms and melodramas. In centers of gay culture – in certain neighborhoods of major cities, but also in media production – "queer culture," or at least gay male culture, is predominantly portrayed as either mired in muscle and decadence or as mirroring heterosexual relationships. Often one stereotypical image fades into another with the aging of those trying to achieve the ideals; there is no larger critique, no analysis of what is contributing to the commodification and consumption that continues, and no notion of whose interests it ultimately serves. Lifestyle becomes choice, and status is integrated into making the right choice.[7]

In cities and rural areas where *coming out* is still traumatic and dangerous, the norm is the mimicking of heterosexual relationships that becomes complete with a move to the suburbs. Much of the mainstream advertising and literature, queer and straight, is about *owning* the right things, whether it's the right body, exciting sex, fashionable accessories, or children. Mass media, of course, promulgates the norms of the dominant culture and the economic machine that creates the desires of consumption. Consumer products encourage the achievement of identity through accessorized lifestyles. In a strange way the acquisition of consumables thus become symbolically equated with the achievement of rights. There is very little difference in the advertising directed toward the straight and the queer markets: whether we look at underwear ads created for gay men or pedophilic images of thin young women produced for the heterosexual market, their intention is the same – they are meant to sell products.[8]

Desire is as much about conforming as it is about biological urges. To see that physical desire can be socially influenced we need only to see that the periodically repeated "scientific" surveys of attraction that would have us believe that European physical features are and (presumably) always have been the yardstick by which sexual desire is measured are patently and wholly ideological. We know that these aspects of culture change across cultures and over time.[9] These "scientific findings," passed on as fact, assume that globalization has not had an effect on the creation of desire, or that mass media are not involved. Patently racist, Euro-centric, and based on class, they feed an ideal of consumer behavior that ranges from lust for designer clothing to the election to have cosmetic surgery.

If we conclude that culture involves social norms by which people experience their daily lives, we next need to consider the means by which these norms are generated. Culture appears by and as social interaction and this interlinking is responsive to flows of energy that exist at any particular moment. Nation-states, for example, can appear as self-generated personalities that encompass the people within them. They generate anthropomorphic representations of themselves that are encompassed in our relationship to them. Commodities, as the driving product of capitalism, need to be continually reproduced and consumed to generate profit, and thus needs must be re-generated. Within this context there is a continuous need in our culture to create the new. Newness is the foundation of desirability, and a culture of newness creates and sells commodities. Novelty functions as the object of desire and thus itself becomes a form of equity.

The drive for newness, for replacement and novelty, does not take place solely in the realm of *things*, even as it attempts to turn feelings into things. Although commodities can take on a social life of their own (such as the symbolic connection between a thing and the social well-being this represents[10]), they do so in the realm of the creation of ideas about living. The generation of consumer need and the attempts by individuals to meet those needs redirects energy away from the recognition of inequality and dominance to the satisfaction of felt desire.

Sexuality and desire have thus been massively consumerized. Roland Barthes (1990) showed us that "The Look" is more important than the act itself. But what does this mean on a cultural *and* on a strictly economic level? Who creates the images of the desirable and how are they played out? Who creates consumption?

The creation of ideal behavior in capitalist societies is basic to social control. Striving to *obtain* commodities fixes energy on the acquisition of things as perceived needs. This, of course, does not rule out a rejection of the creation of need; but it does lead to inequalities that are reinforced by that very act of striving.

Advertising, as Stuart Ewen (1976; 1988) explains, is a form of social production designed to reinforce existing institutionalized roles. Its roots lie in the socialization of successive immigrant groups who, while experiencing the shock of factory life, were made to feel uncomfortable for what they didn't possess (decent people, so the messages went, don't live without washing machines and polished fingernails). Even the 1920 edition of the *Encyclopedia of the Social Sciences* proposed that

> What is needed for American consumption, is training in art and taste in a generous consumption of goods, if such there can be. Advertizing is the greatest force at work against the traditional economy of an age-long poverty as well as that of our own pioneer period; it is almost the only force at work against Puritanism in consumption. It can infuse art into the things of life, and it will.

Advertising then, as today, capitalized on the feelings of helplessness and alienation brought on by industrialization and the separation of the control of production from the producers. It is a means of social discipline.[11] It necessarily leads to disappointment, for the drive in capitalism constantly to increase accumulation produces new goods that continually change the rules of the game. What is desirable today is tomorrow's kitsch. Stainless steel bathroom fixtures, thirties-style dinnerware, soaps, and styles of lighting, are presently fashionable. They will soon be replaced by new fashions, more desirable objects. As laborers, we not only create products, the products create us.

In their famous studies of "Middletown" (1937; [1929] 1956), the Lynds made the important observation that "Members of the working class address their activities by giving their living primarily to *things*, using material tools in the making of things and the performance of services, while members of [the business class] address their activities to *people* in the selling or promotion of things, services and ideas" ([1929] 1956: 147).[12] While the distinction between those creating need and those consuming it are more complex (for those who create also consume), the recognition that products are not only consumed but also *made* by labor raises the issue of class in a direct way.

The integration of advertising and consumerism into the psyche is a multi-layered process, mediated by a dominant "culture-ideology" (Sklair, 1998: 297). The seeding of the unconscious by social processes such as advertising acts to mask the etiology of desire, sexual or otherwise, which underpins consumer culture. Our desires, directed by cultural and ideological phenomena such as advertising, thus respond to the norms used as baselines for conformity. In such a way, our wishes to conform, to "pass," to be a part of a larger community, *to have an identity*, are channeled into the grooves laid out for us by mass media.

Queer writing has not addressed the assumption of uniformity in needs and desires. References to the Fire Island scene, and the communities of Cherry Grove, Key West, West Hollywood, or the Hamptons are about class and status as much as they are about the creation of identity.[13] There is a certain schizophrenia operating here: what the history of advertising shows is that you can appeal to the queer community without condoning its behavior. While the need for community enhances the drive for conformity, the realization of the generalized non-acceptance and "otherness" of queerness fuels arguments for difference while it excites the desire to "normalize" and consume, evoking courses of action that often result in the buying of uniforms rather than the celebrating of difference.

## Globalizing queer

The globalization of capitalism and the economic forces that sustain it have necessarily led to the globalization of queer culture, and to the different vectors of hierarchy that are present in cultures around the world. Multinational trade and investment agreements are indicative of the opposing forces of labor and capital that are now omnipresent in every aspect of life around the globe. There is a popular assumption that as global economic forces predominate, diversity will be lessened by the overpowering forms of dominance that effectively destroy cultures much as they do forms of labor organization. But as Nash writes, "I would argue for the perpetuation and even intensification of cultural variability with the spread of industrialization and modernization. While larger clusters of shared traits tend to be atomized, variation in the frequency of associated traits increases" (1981: 412). In other words, peoples and cultures often integrate cultural traits, existing and new, into unified beliefs and behavior, maintaining their own shared systems of belief. In the process the imposing traits are transformed.[14] It is this variability that serves as the basis of continued identity and as one basis for resistance to domination. We thus should not assume that because multinationals have managed to globalize their strategies the resulting homogenization in the productive management of capital creates homogenization in the wider culture. This imposition may be challenged and resisted in ways that are both similar to and different from resistance movements in the most capital-intensive countries. On the other hand, the shops of Madison Avenue in New York can be found in any major city in the world. The consumers who can afford to buy these products are themselves transnationally mobile: people who identify more with those of their same status around the globe than with their local communities.

Like other aspects of race, class, and gender, the conceptions of sexuality in cultures around the world beyond the heterosexual have begun to influence the meaning of "queer." Dennis Altman cites the case of a Filipino anthropologist, who, after having extensively studied in the United States, "still identifies with the *bakla* (effeminate homosexuals) of his native town" (1996: 77). Yet "queer," in the sense of a sophisticated (mostly white male) consumer culture, can also be found around the globe and presents a picture of homogenization that defies local variability. The danger of ignoring local responses to the opening up (or rejecting) of forms of sexuality is that we miss the true sense of the difference that exists to reinforce identity. But Altman's assumption that the globalization of the gay identity is universal is contradicted by his own recognition that indigenous assumptions about gender and sexuality do not necessarily correspond with Western ones, and that they persist even in the face of encroachment by Western culture.[15]

In the United States and the other advanced capitalist countries, the "market" can overpower legal restrictions on the definition of morality. The market has picked up the pace of partial acceptance where the positive effect of negative labeling has left off, and it defines and provides continuity of identity communities that can afford the products advertising sells.

The struggle for freedom to choose one's gender and sexuality takes place in the same political sphere as the capitalist enterprise and the generation of inequality. The inclusion of sexual rights by the drafters of the new South African constitution involved a clearly delineated exposition of prejudice, exploitation, and discrimination that had been the result of a powerful historical experience. The existence of new forms of industrial expansion as expressed by ever-emerging trade and investment agreements, and the effects of these (both negative and positive) on configurations of sexuality, as well as on conditions for the basic sustenance of human life, are ongoing concerns. The generation of conflict around the globe, be it ethnic, racial, gendered, or otherwise, is intensified by managerial strategies to streamline the accumulation of capital and the attempted conditioning of beliefs and behavior that it requires. The means by which these forces work themselves out in varying contexts remains to be explored.

# 5 Meta-identity, performativity, and internalized homophobia

> I began with the speculative question of whether feminist politics could do without a "subject" in the category of women. At stake is not whether it still makes sense, strategically or transitionally, to refer to women in order to make representational claims on their behalf.
>
> (Butler, 1990: Conclusion)

Queer theory promotes the "self" of the individual as an alternative to wider social interaction. This focus, as I argue, is closely tied to the development of late capitalist ideology, where the individual becomes both signifier and signified, disassembling the social ties that bind communities together.

As a consequence, the overriding constraint of Queer theory is the unwillingness of its authors to investigate the relationship between individuals and society. The self as non-conformist becomes part of a stance that disengages politics as a reality of daily life.

Why this focus instead of another? I have explored the perception that the social movements of the 1960s and 1970s did not adequately address distinctions among exploited populations, and the role this lack of recognition has played in the derivation and acceptance of theories of difference. But as I have also stated, the bounded individual, as "self," *different and unique*, cannot be the center of strategies for social change.

## Academic stardom, performance, and the attributes of language

If there is an individual who has come to embody Queer theory, it is Judith Butler. She has come to represent, and has accepted the position of, a leading-edge theorist. While it will be easy to argue that I do not adequately engage the complex epistemology of Butler's work here, I nonetheless do address the implications and consequences of her assumptions, including the role of politics for queer communties. I do not believe that it is Butler's intention to regress theory to a conservative self-directed individualism; yet all the conceptual elements of individualism are present in her work, and what a theory implies about practice is, in my view, more pertinent for our times than conjectural musing.

Commenting on some of the arguments presented by her critics, Butler writes that

> Perhaps you are already wondering how it is that I might take the time to rehearse these arguments in this way, giving them air-time, as it were, and perhaps you are also wondering whether or not I am already parodying these positions. Do I think that they are worthless, or do I think that they are important, deserving of a response? If I were parodying these positions, that might imply that I think that they are ridiculous, hollow, formulaic, that they have a currency as discourse that allows for them to be taken up by almost anyone and to sound convincing, even if delivered by the most improbable person.
>
> But what if my rehearsal involves a temporary identification with them, even as I myself participate in the cultural politics under attack? Is that temporary identification that I perform, the one that raises the question of whether I am involved in a parody of these positions, not precisely a moment in which, for better or worse, they become my position?
>
> (1998: 33–34)

It is often difficult to work out whether Butler is presenting a parodied position or not, given her controversial writing style. She has argued that complex thoughts require complex writing, insinuating that it is the reader who is to blame if the style appears too complex readily to understand what is being put forward (Butler, 1999).

But let us recall Marx's critique of the "subjectivists" in *The German Ideology*: "First of all an abstraction is made from a fact; then it is declared that the fact is based on an abstraction ... That is how to proceed if you want to appear ... profound and speculative" (Marx, 1939: 114–115).

Beyond the positioning, Butler's writing represents a level of analysis that ignores on-the-ground activity. It is one thing to imply – as Butler does, following Foucault – that power is omnipresent and cannot be discussed in general terms. It is another to ignore power as the site of oppression. By dismissing power and its genesis, her discussion precludes any real proposals for change. Not surprisingly, she offers none.

Butler's argument with her critics is that her work has been relegated to the level of the "merely cultural" (Butler, 1998). She reasons that placing her work in this domain creates the same divisions between material and cultural that the "left" has sought to resolve. Butler's larger critique of new social movements – that they have been militated against by a mysterious and unlocated "hegemonic left" that represents a new social conservatism – dismisses the history of left politics as an amorphous whole (1998: 36).[1] This is indeed a surprising assumption, suspiciously regressive in its own right. It insults a long history of union activism, movements against imperialism and colonialism, and the fights for equality that she purports to defend.

Marx and his followers, of course, never saw the cultural and material as a binary system, consistently referring to the effect of culture on economic functioning and of the economy on culture. Marx and Engels did emphasize the role of reproduction in the maintenance of society, of labor as an *activity* integral to human *being*, or "sensuous activity." But it was not meant to minimize the role of humans as social animals who create culture: "Circumstances make men just as men make circumstances" (Marx and Engels, 1939: 29). This statement indicates a methodology that is dialectical rather than linear, or as Mészaros puts it,

> And here we come to a crucial question: the complexity of Marx's dialectical methodology. In a mechanical conception there is no clear-cut line of demarcation between "determined" and its "determinants." Not so within the framework of dialectical methodology. In terms of the latter, although the economic foundations of capitalist society constitute the "ultimate determinants" of the social being of its classes, these "ultimate *determinants*" are at the same time also "*determined* determinants." In other words, Marx's assertions about the ontological significance of economics become meaningful only if we are able to grasp his idea of "*complex interactions*" in the most varied fields of human activity. Accordingly, the various institutional and intellectual manifestations of human life are not simply "built upon" an economic basis, but also actively *structure* the latter through the immensely intricate and relatively autonomous structure of their own. "Economic determinations" do not exist outside the historically changing complex of specific mediations, including the most "*spiritual*" ones.
>
> (Mészaros, 1971: 145)

The separating of these components misses their interdependence. Yet despite Butler's claim that she unites the material with the cultural, the focus of her work is on the deconstruction of the abstract: on categories, identities, and speech. These phenomena are only part of the mechanisms of daily life that sustain production and reproduction.

Butler is against the identification of herself or others with categories of being that have been the baseline for social movements (1993a: 307). Susan Wolfe and Julia Penelope (1993), representing a growing discomfort with this kind of widely adapted position, warn against the tendency to invalidate identities, problematic as they may seem. Dismissing the identity, particularly of oppressed groups, relegates them to invisibility in the same way that Butler claims left-oriented theory does. It renders them invisible and therefore unable to construct the resistance necessary to counter the cruelty of lived experiences. If there is a comfortable consensus that we cannot quite define queer except as *separate from* the established dominant order, then there cannot be identity, however temporary.

The building of theory that works against active collective resistance fits well within what the anthropologist Laura Nader terms the production of "cohesive harmony" (Nader, 1990). While asserting the right to difference, it is a phenomenon "against the contentious in anything, and it has very strange bedfellows, from people with various psychiatric therapy movements, Christian fundamentalists, corporations sick of paying lawyers, activists who believe we should love each other ... and it's spread into different parts of American life." It is a perception that says, "If you disagree, you should really keep your mouth shut" (Cockburn, 1995: 93).

This principle is backed by the fear of economic and social retaliation and has been effectively used in the culture wars between government and communities, where trade-offs are made that are called compromises while in fact working to the benefit of those controlling production. It resonates strongly with the cost-accounting approach, and with current American cultural values. And it has gained scientific credibility. In a 1985 issue of *Science*, Daniel Koshland coined one such compromise as the "undesirability principle." In his formula, given that some industries would like to dump toxic waste at lowest possible costs, that environmental groups would like to place severe restraints on that dumping, and that consumers desire to purchase the products of industry at the lowest possible prices, society can obtain a goal that satisfies all contending groups by adjusting the relative costs. But the level of accumulation is not the only place where this ideology has been successfully employed. Certainly the "don't ask – don't tell" policy of the Clinton administration towards gays in the military is another example of a subjugation that appears on the surface to be progressive, but has dire consequences for self-actualization and identity. The "harmony" this allows becomes no more than the hegemony it creates, as the promises made to queer communities by candidates for office are all but disregarded when those same candidates assume office. It is the consequence of alliances based on "having" rather than resisting.

Butler acknowledges that the academy, by designating arenas of study, separates race from sexuality, class from ethnicity, and so on, contending that these are the very categories the "left" hopes to transcend (1998: 35). But it does not follow that they should then be abandoned. What she does not consider are the mechanics of social control that work against the production of theory in the academy that includes an account of the genesis of oppression.

Butler offers that the attempt to integrate the analysis of resistance with forms of oppression will result in more factionalization (1998: 34). She arrives at this assumption by highlighting the "I" rather than the structural attributes of capital and class.[2] Ironically, if not logically, this representation of "queer" in the academy has provided for a depoliticizing effect. In Suzanna Walters' words,

> One of the interesting aspects of this phenomenon in the academy is that you do not have to be queer to do it, in fact it is better if you are not. *Queer* (as opposed to gay or lesbian), lets you off the identity hook the way that gender studies has vis-á-vis women's studies, while cashing in on the trendiness of postmodernism.
>
> (Walters, 1996: 840)

Thus, the academy has mimicked the ideological reproduction of difference that late capitalism favors. In like fashion, Pierre Bourdieu, commenting on the current period of neo-conservative reconstruction in which we now find ourselves, wonders,

> What, I will be asked, is the role of intellectuals in all this? I make no attempt to list – it would take too long and be too cruel – all the forms of default or, worse still, collaboration. I need only mention the arguments of so-called modern and postmodern philosophers who, when not content with leaving well alone and burying themselves in scholastic games, restrict themselves to verbal defense of reason and rational dialogue, or, worse still, suggest an allegedly postmodern but actually radical-chic version of the ideology of the end of ideologies, complete with the condemnation of grand narratives and a nihilistic denunciation of science.
>
> (Bourdieu, 1998: 227)

Butler announces that "*queer politics is regularly figured by the orthodoxy as the cultural extreme of politicization*" (1998: 38; emphasis in the original). While "orthodoxy" is not defined, it is presumed to be the "hegemonic left," and she again does not comment on what constitutes "politics." The possible implication that this hegemony in the form of orthodoxy is found on the left rather than the right is a dangerous signal that the argument is taking place in the wrong arena.

Moreover, many of Butler's answers to her critics are not responses at all: they are further deconstructions of abstract positions. She goes so far as to define class in terms of burdens, arguing that those with HIV and AIDS constitute a differential class based on their access to health care.[3] While she agrees that the material and the cultural cannot be artificially separated, she performs exactly this analytical function as she focuses her attention on the "cultural" realm, thereby collapsing material reproduction. She wonders in her conclusion to "Merely Cultural?" whether by criticizing her, we are

perhaps witnessing a scholarly effort to ameliorate the political force of

queer struggles by refusing to see the fundamental shift in the conceptualizing and institutionalizing of social relations that they demand? Is the association of the sexual with the cultural, and the concomitant effort to render
autonomous and degrade the cultural sphere, the unthinking response to a
sexual degradation perceived to be happening within the cultural sphere, an
effort to colonize and contain homosexuality in and as the cultural itself?[4]

(Butler, 1998: 44)

Beyond the use of a language of radical politics for the sake of argument, there
is no analysis of "political force" or "queer struggles." What we are led to perceive
is that they are non-economic, and that while political struggles may upset
capitalist relations of production, the struggles themselves do not have to be
directed at those relationships. By transforming *ideas* of sexuality and gender
through personal struggle, it is inferred that the rest will follow. This approach is
a natural continuation of the theories developed by postmodernists such as
Foucault and Baudrillard as a reaction to the movements of the 1960s, previously
discussed. We are left to imagine that the most radical struggles are with
ourselves, and that with further consciousness-raising they will produce social
change.

The missing links do not go unnoticed. In a response to Butler, Nancy Fraser
(1998) makes the observation that "misrecognition is an institutionalized social
relation, not a psychological state" (1998: 141). Although Fraser's objections are
stated in reference to *status*-based societies – and thus she misses the dimensions
of pre-capitalist egalitarian community relations – she recognizes that the "base-
superstructural" model has been overplayed and that any discussion based upon it
feeds the same misconceptions and forms of logic that need to be reordered.
Unfortunately, Fraser accepts the erroneous assumption made by Mauss and Lévi-
Strauss that women are primarily commodities in pre-capitalist societies, but she
does recognize that historicization "represents a better approach to social theory
than destabilization or deconstruction" (1998: 149). Micaela Di Leonardo (1993)
makes a stronger point by reasserting that the "political" is not separate from the
"economic." She believes that the postmodernism and post-structuralism that
Butler and her peers practice is in itself a kind of disciplinary colonization, where
the practitioners of a field of academia have simply accepted their own arguments
as true and necessary and subsumed other discussion. Ideologies need to be
contextualized, and we cannot "escape our political and economic placement at
home" (1993: 78). The historical and ethnographic fallacies presented in defense
of the postmodernist and post-structuralist critique aside, it is doubtful that it
would exist at all without a new political juncture of fragmentation that Rorty
(1991) and Jameson (1991) both note is being produced in late capitalism, and
which Haraway (1985) and Eagleton (1986) point to as having led to a new stage
in politics.

Ellen Wood (1986) asserts that the production of postmodernist and post-structuralist theory is based on unacknowledged but specific class interests. A class analysis means a "comprehensive analysis of social relations and power ... based on the historical/materialist principle which places the relations of production at the center of social life and regards their exploitative character as the root of social and political oppression" (Wood, 1986: 14). Such an analysis does not mean overlooking " 'the differences which express the social formation' " as Marx put it, nor a mechanistic materialism, but it maintains that oppression finds its most extreme and violent expression through economic exploitation and alienation (Marx, 1978: 247; Stabile, 1994: 48). Carole Stabile further critiques postmodernist theory as

> those forms of critical theory that rely upon an uncritical and idealist focus on the discursive constitution of "the real," a positivistic approach to the notion of "difference," and a marked lack of critical attention to the context of capitalism and their own locations within processes of production and reproduction.
>
> (1994: 52)

"For example," she continues, "against the Marxist centrality of class struggle, and in an ironic if unintentional mirroring of the mercurial nature of capitalism, Michel Foucault argues: 'But if it is against *power* that one struggles, then all those who acknowledge it as intolerable can begin the struggle wherever they find themselves and in terms of their own activity (or passivity)' " (1994: 49).

Former Marxist theorists such as Ernesto Laclau and Chantal Mouffe have even come to agree with current postmodern and post-structuralist formulations that the centrality of a class analysis in Marxist theory is "essentialist," and that Marxism requires a new center (1985). They suggest that capitalism should not be conceptualized as a system, but as an articulation, which is, they say,

> the construction of modal points which partially fix meaning ... the partial character of this fixation proceeds from the openness of the social, a result, in its turn, of the constant overflowing of every discourse by the infinitude of the field of discursivity.
>
> (Laclau and Mouffe, 1985: 113)

Thus, they say, Marxism privileges "class" over other forms of oppression that are not constituted economically. As Stabile (1994) notes, however, the examples they provide are "generally middle-class movements ... One is obliged to ask who it is, precisely, that Laclau and Mouffe's argument privileges as the agents of social change ... Or to put it in slightly more pointed terms, whose political interests are served by their theory of nonfixity and discursive equivalences?", leaving her to conclude,

> who better to form the new center for political struggle than intellectuals –
> so that we get the privileging of intellectuals rather than the privileging of
> class: what this results in is a convenient move, for (a) we don't need to
> invoke the notion of class at all because the concept is intrinsically essential-
> ist; and (b) we do not need to concern ourselves with the class privilege
> enjoyed by intellectuals since oppressions are, within the discursive field,
> necessarily unfixed and somehow equivalent.
>
> (Stabile, 1994: 50–51)

Butler, of course, would not agree: she places herself and her analyses in "a position that places itself beyond the play of power, and which seeks to establish the meta-political basis for a negotiation of power relations that is perhaps the most insidious ruse of power" (Butler, 1992: 4). But what could possibly be "meta-political" in any real sense, except, perhaps, "meta-identity"? Are the politics of inequality somehow unreal, not based on actual access to resources? In the end, Butler's theory of "politics as such" runs on the same conceptual ground as Foucault, who Stuart Hall argues "saves for himself 'the political' with his insistence on power" but denies himself *a politics* because he has no idea of the "relations of force" (Hall, 1986: 349). In sum, Butler is unwilling to deal with power outside of the limited boundaries of the academy, where she admits the power of older academics and tenured professors is at least observable.

## Roles and subversions: professing parody

Judith Butler has expressed her position most influentially in the elaboration of a theory of performativity, which asserts that because all categories and identities only exist in the ideal, all attempts to reconcile the ideal with the real result in performance. Gender is a representation, and, at the same time, that very representation of gender is its construction.

But the projection of ideals is a consequence of the relationships of power: the ideal posits the expected norms. The purveyors of capitalism have been very successful at providing strategies to accomplish this goal through advertising and by promoting ethics that make people believe that, as individuals, they are not reaching their full potential. Resistance may take place in the form of working against the ideal – or parodying it – as in drag, but it is important to recognize that this form of resistance does not actually confront the ideal on the political level. It resists neither the creation of the ideal nor those who create it.

Entering through the backdoor of resistance studies and anti- or neo-structuralist positions, performativity theory addresses itself to the problems of idealized norms within systems. It emphasizes forced and forceful reiterations rather than the intrinsic meaning of acts. The presumption is that gender is something people act out. Gender is not an inherent quality that people possess. Butler argues that people mistake the acts for the essence and, in the process, come to believe that they are mandatory (Morris, 1995: 573; cf. Butler, 1993a).

The premise of performativity is that this imitation allows for subversive acts. By asserting that the body assumes its gender in the culturally mandated practices of everyday life, the theory of gender performativity offers the possibility of going against the expected.

Gender is simply considered the continuing of a process of subjective rendering. In other words, gender is made up and idealized in a way that no one can actually *be* that category. But as Rosalind Morris (1995) suggests, this elucidation of gender roles has caused the categories of sex and gender to be reduced to subjective experience. When gender is examined cross-culturally, a clearer picture emerges. As I have suggested, much of the theory that has questioned non-normative gender finds its examples in extraordinary cases, such as the "institutionalized transvestitism" of the Kathoey of Thailand (Morris, 1995: 569). Or it looks to societies where gender is explicitly marked by rites of passage. What Morris correctly asks is:

> What kinds of questions does the theory of discursive or performative gender seek to answer that the notion of ambiguity can provide so potent and all-encompassing an explanation? What social and historical forces are implicated in this discourse, and finally, what might be its consequences?
>
> (1995: 570)

Morris identifies two tendencies in the ethnographic literature: one that gender is arbitrary but determining; the other that it is constructed, identifiable, and given by history. The first tendency, which concentrates on how cultures construct gender and create subjects, is the anthropology of difference (1995: 573). It focuses on rites of passage where gender is publicly marked. She calls the second tendency the anthropology of decomposing difference, which focuses on institutions of ambiguity, encompassing everything from institutionalized transgendering in non-Western societies to specifically framed gestures of parody and transgression in North American theatre.

Given that the social construction is most visible when it deviates from the dominant ideology that created it, then it is appropriate that the work on performance focuses on cases of seemingly ambiguous genders, whether they be institutionalized, such as the Berdache or the Hijras, or temporary and theatricalized acts. Morris suggests that the most serious failure of the analytical work on these events is that it often confuses ritual as reiteration with ritual as an originating act (1995: 576). If ritual is reiteration, or performance, where does the non-normative act come from? Marilyn Strathern, for example, describes the seclusion of Daulo girls, and the ritual initiation that takes place during that period, as a transformation that moves the individual from a non-sexed to a sexed person. But she also

> makes a good case for considering these kinds of ritual processes (and the ethnographic literature is bursting with accounts of them) as a general mode of fragmentation, in which sexually whole and in some senses individual persons, namely children, are socialized into relations and dependencies of kinship, age, sexuality and gender.
>
> (Morris, 1995: 578)

If socialization, then, reinforces gendered relationships among individuals and within society, is the act of subversion necessarily positive? Is performance, understood as individualized, if not an individual act, conducive to developing movements for social change? What do subverted roles represent?

For Butler, drag as subverted role confronts and parodies normative gender roles. But normative is inexact here, since we note that all gender roles are attempts at playing or at reaching impossible goals. There is no origin here and no baseline. All gender activity is then explicable only in its own terms: nothing is original and everything is original. It is from this premise that Butler can claim that those who charge that drag queens, butches, and femmes are derivatives of the heterosexual norm are homophobic, since they are operating with the assumption that heterosexuality is the fundamental axis by which all else is judged (Butler, 1993a: 313). But in a society that *does* discriminate against those who do not exhibit heterosexual "normality," is it possible to claim that heterosexuality is not the baseline?

Not only do our culture, our socialization, and our experiences constitutionally influence our behavior, but we also react according to the terms of our culture. In asserting that all gender roles are copies, and therefore that each has the same degree of originality (in that they are *different* from each other), there is an inferred refusal to create meaningful connections that make for observable realities. Moreover, the notion that these differences represent subversion is only part of the story. Drag and other role subversions can symbolize and play out a wide variety of affects, feelings, connections, and misconceptions. They can be hostile or they can be accommodating. They can also display an internalized homophobia that derives from a fear to identify and connect. Fear is fundamentally distinct from a refusal to engage. It may, however, have the same result.

According to Butler, "*In imitating gender, drag implicitly reveals the imitative structure of gender itself – as well as its contingency*" (1991: 137). Acknowledging the referential aspects of the performance, she continues, "Although the gender meanings taken up in these parodic styles are clearly part of hegemonic, misogynist culture, they are nevertheless denaturalized and mobilized through their parodic recontextualization" (1991: 138). Why? Are their referential aspects different from the aspects of behavior they mimic? Or is gender, as performance, in fact meta-naturalized and fetishized? The objections of many in the feminist movement to aspects of male-to-female drag, in particular, are not about the exhibition of false consciousness. They are reacting to representations of women as over-stylized *things*, as commodities that are produced in the same misogynist culture Butler claims it parodies. The flirtatious anger often found in the subculture of drag is certainly not a clean "parody." It is a very real anger generated by the oppression that constitutes the construction of gender. To make matters more disturbing, *drag is primarily a working class phenomenon and/or phenomenon of the disenfranchised*. The "houses" characteristic of lifestyle drag queens, the pageants displayed by these houses, and the butch-femme bar scene of major cities are not as a rule populated by those who have had the opportunities of education, money, and free-willed consumption. An inability to hire lawyers and actively resist personal oppression is documented in examples in recollections such as Leslie Feinberg's *Transgender Warriors* (1996), where in a story of the interaction between a young Butch and an older Femme, the Butch asks the Femme if she is strong enough. She answers: "Nobody's strong enough. You just get through it, the best you can. Butches like you [and Al] don't have a choice. It's gonna happen too. You just gotta try and live through it" (Feinberg, 1996).

For further contrast, we can ask: what is the nature of blackface? What of mainstream beauty pageants? Blackface *is* subversive to a general rendering of equality among races; beauty pageants *are* subversive to the fight against the objectification of bodies. But if parody is simply the data that tells us gender roles are imitations of nothing in particular, then where do we go from there? Bodies, as Stockton (1996) remarks, become separate from the constructions that render them. But how do you parody an imitation? How is the imitation concretized and experienced on the ground? Butler does say (as an aside) that parody in itself is not subversive (1991: 139). But she never answers the following question: what does it actually represent?

Despite nominal lip service, Butler disregards the differences inherent in societies based on class and the differences between class and non-class-based societies. We cannot equate the economic and cultural contexts of drag and the phenomenon of birdache. The latter comes from a historical context of pre-class configurations, while the former is firmly rooted in mass consumerism. Consider that parody in the form of drag has been integrated into mainstream Hollywood culture as fashion: films like *Priscilla, Queen of the Desert*, *Foo Man Chu*, and the delicate *Tootsie* may at first appear as presenting characters who behave in ways that are contrary to expected roles. *In fact, however, all of these examples assert stereotypes of gender rather than subvert them*. They all acknowledge diversity and yet reveal it to be in need of control. They are not necessarily anti-homophobic, but, as Walters clarifies, they may be quite the opposite (1996: 857).

If we concede that a non-acceptance of expectation (should we know what that is), rejecting the ideal (again not clearly identified), is the only viable and radicalized activity that does not feed into existing structures of power, what precisely does this entail? The idea that performance and parody are radical activities encapsulates a grandiose ambition: if we can convince ourselves that we are making a difference, perhaps we are. After all, the power of positive thinking has been emphasized in US culture for some time – a version of individualism at its most hopeful juncture. Unfortunately, those who control the means and forces of production, who regulate the images we see and promulgate the ideals, are considerably more action-oriented. It is folly to imagine that a combination of Foucaultian understandings of power and a head for fun results in radical activity. Such a politics can be no more than individualized resistance to perceived-as-normative expectations. Soldiers do not exist for abstract reasons, and they will not disappear because we claim them as performance. The notion that women, people of color, or any other minority will be better off obtaining a consciousness that refuses to engage its oppressors ignores the people trying to make sense of their own subjugation.

Performativity, as Butler would have it, is ahistorical, unconnected to specific contexts of culture and time. When boys dressed as women in Shakespeare's plays, they did not subvert cultural renditions of gender. Cultural inversions across time and across cultures cannot be reduced to one and the same phenomenon of "queerness."

## Parody, imitation, and internalized homophobia

There is another, more insidious manifestation of power and culture at work here, one that cannot be recognized under the rubric of Butler's writing because it transgresses her logic. Parody and imitation can just as easily be encountered as an involution of gender roles, as an acceptance of rejection. As anthropologists and psychologists have shown over time, humor and laughter can be just as much a part of the recognition of a painful reality as self-assertive parody. If alienation is a part of the individual's structural experience in capitalist relations, where producers are separated from the end results of their production and from their communities, then the human essence is an abstraction in any individual. In reality, the individual is made up of the ensemble of human relations in which he or she is a part. If, as Butler contends, "Gender is a norm that can never be fully internalized; 'the internal' is a surface signification, and gender norms are finally phantasmatic, impossible to embody" (1991: 141), then the fact of alienated gender is impossible to ignore. Gender becomes an unconnected aspect of existence within present-day society, a place that can be designated, but which cannot be fully experienced. We are all, then, by definition marginalized. This marginalization is expressed in many ways – but more importantly, it is experienced differentially by class position, race, *and* gender. It is also reinforced by prejudice, stigmatization, and violence. The enormous burden of this position is enacted by dis-eases of society: economic instability, psychological trauma, and "cures" that blame the victim. In this reality, gender is not performed but real, and, certainly, a queer reality is different from a heterosexual one.

The dominant culture is more than an abstract idea that posits the forces of oppression. It also causes pain. Hate crimes, the high rate of teenage suicide among queers, and job and economic discrimination all lead to psychological states that overshadow any acts of parody and imitation. It is not surprising that anger is invoked. Furthermore, the exclusion of this actuality posits an uncomfortable question about performativity theory in general. If resistance is located in the self, if parody and imitation are deemed subversive, and if this qualifies as more useful than active community-linked resistance, what are the consequences? Parody ends up looking more like a product of fear than political strategy. Consider Butler's doubts about "coming out:"

> The discourse of "coming out" has clearly served its purposes, but what are its risks? And here I am not speaking of unemployment or public attack or violence, which are quite clearly and widely on the increase against those who are perceived as "out" whether or not of their own design. Is the "subject" who is "out" free of its subjection and finally in the clear? Or could it be that the subjection that subjectivates the gay or lesbian subject in some ways continues to oppress, or oppresses most insidiously, once "outness" is claimed? What or who is it that is "out," made manifest and fully disclosed, when and if I reveal myself as a lesbian? What is it that is now known, anything? What remains permanently concealed by the very linguistic act that offers up the promise of a transparent revelation of sexuality? Can sexuality even remain sexuality once it submits to a criterion of transparency and disclosure, or does it perhaps cease to be sexuality precisely when the semblance of full explicitness is achieved? Is sexuality of any kind even possible without that opacity designated by the unconscious, which means simply that the conscious "I" who would reveal its sexuality is perhaps the last to know the meaning of what it says?
>
> (Butler, 1993a: 309)

Observing that Butler's questioning of whether "sexuality [can] even remain sexuality once it submits to a criterion of transparency and disclosure," Suzanna Walters wryly remarks that

> Hmm, that old devil moon is back again. Sexuality, she must be, how you say,

an enigma, hidden, dark, unconscious for her to be … fun. Shhh, don't talk, don't know, don't even think you know, don't claim, don't reveal: desire needs dark curtains of mystery to be pleasurable.

(Walters, 1996: 852)

"Queer" in this sense, then, attempts to dissolve sexuality and annuls the basis for sexual identity, precluding a confrontation with a morality that dictates sexual correctness, affirming some practices while stigmatizing others. "Worse," as Lee Siegel writes, "it often seems that calling oneself queer is a tactic for not acknowledging that one is merely gay, for not shouldering the burdens of coming out or the responsibilities that come with accepting the inevitable reality of a sexual identity and getting on with the rest of life" (1998: 34).

If we do not "come out," we cannot identify our sexuality or gender in the sense of knowing exactly who we are. This knowing is impossible without identifying with others engaged in a similar struggle. Since it is, in fact, impossible to constitute a movement for social change based on individual self-ness, we must ask ourselves what or who Butler's position benefits. To see one's gender identity as imitation or parody is to view the self as unreal. It distances the actor from a confrontation with the objects of oppression and thwarts any resistance that matters. It is individual difference reified to the exclusion of community. When we are not comfortable enough with our positions to seek out others who are in the same position, and to use this identity, our identification with them, to counter the symbolic and real violence that exists, we are also hiding from ourselves the real discrimination that denies self-assertion and fulfillment. The result is a fear of engagement, a true manifestation of an internalized homophobia that rests on the individual's rejection of identity and of power, the refusal to identify and to engage power, and thus the rejection of labels.

To have a label that is not accepted as equal to others in this culture is to be "less-than," producing marginalization and *shame* for those desiring to be on an equal par. Here marginality can become an identity in itself: if one recognizes and embraces the fact that one is marginalized, then there is no need to seek support. This position declares that the only way to prevent being eaten by power is to reject participation, "to disclaim," a pessimistic stance that reinforces rejection.

Denying a label or an identity is far easier than a fight for equity that might fail, thus rendering the individual even more isolated. By denying the identification and the material fact of labeling, shame is thus avoided and no real resistance is actualized. But in fact the individual becomes even more alone.

Judith Butler concludes her discussion of gender and its troubles with a discussion of a politics that defies the necessity of a subject. Since individuals continually negotiate their roles and existences, she claims that there is no substantive and identifiable "I" that can form the basis for identification. In the true Heideggerian sense, "Being" is beyond articulation. "To understand identity is a *practice*," Butler notes, "and as a signifying practice, it is to understand culturally untelligible subjects as the resulting effects of a rule-bound discourse that inserts itself in the pervasive and mundane signifying acts of linguistic life" (1991: 145). Asserting that the deconstruction of identity is not the deconstruction of politics, she nonetheless posits only one politicized strategy:

> Practices of parody can serve to reengage and reconsolidate the very distinction between a privileged and naturalized gender configuration and one that appears as derived, phantasmatic, and mimetic – a failed copy, as it were. And surely parody has been used to further a politics of despair, one which affirms a seemingly inevitable exclusion of marginal genders from the territory of the natural and the real.
>
> (Butler, 1991: 146)

# Part III

# Moving ahead

# 6    From culture to action

We know that homosexuality is defined in the sphere of dominant ideological relations as a deviant form of heterosexuality, whether those who would deconstruct heterosexuality as a concept would have it or not. Heterosexuality, by contrast, does not require homosexuality for its own definition in popular thought. Because there is no analysis of this asymmetry on the horizon in the postmodernist direction, the way in which heterosexuality is asserted as the only correct and dominant social form is never pursued.

Queerness as a deviant form of heterosexuality results in oppression. When this fact is not confronted, it can lead to maladaptive responses that include the markings of internalized homophobia: depression, psychosis, resignation, and apathy. These are very much reactions to the ways in which we view ourselves, which in turn are, at least in part, due to the ways in which we are constantly told to view ourselves. Here, the production of consciousness takes a very concrete form. Those enduring this form of violence cannot, even in the academy, simply decide to disengage. We cannot simply refuse to acknowledge these facts of social life in our present society, and hope that our circumstances will change. Although the lack of definition is what has inspired the use of "queer," it cannot, as Butler herself asserts, "overcome its constituent history of injury" (1993b: 223).

Be that as it may, "queer," as put forward by Queer theorists, has no inherent historical or social context. We continually return to the following question: to whom does it belong and what does it represent? These advocates of "queer" do not acknowledge that *queer* is produced by social relations, and therefore contains the attributes of existing social relations.

As I have shown, Queer theory, particularly as it is expressed in Butler's writings on performativity, dichotomizes the political as personal and the political as social action into a binary that positions political action in impossible terms. The nature of the "political" is never clearly discussed, and remains a chasm (cf. Kaufman and Martin, 1994).

However appealing the notion of positioning the self through a reinterpretation of the "I" may be, it is misguided as political action: it cannot generate the collective energy and organization necessary to challenge existing structures of power. As Michael Aglietta observes, "There is no magical road where the most abstract concepts magically command the movement of society" (1979: 43). The question of politics, then, brings us back to where we began: what is the nature of the political and how do we address it? Is it beneficial to maintain alliances with established political parties? Can we adopt the dominant values of our culture and still hope to change the dynamics of those values? How do we form alliances with other oppressed groups? Is there a structural economic basis for such an alliance, or should we look elsewhere? Perhaps most importantly: is it possible, given the tremendous resources represented by the dominant and coercive ideology of our present social relations, to maintain the energy necessary to develop and continue modes of resistance that counter it? In the last question, as I will show, lies an answer to the issue of alliances and structural identification. But first, we need to refocus the discussion.

## What is political?

In March of 1999, the Multilateral Agreement on Investment (MAI) was derailed in Paris. Consumer, environmental, and labor organizations leaked its secretive negotiations over the Internet, and the terms of the Agreement provoked world-wide protest. Like the progressively protective strategies for transnational corporations passed by the General Agreement on Treaties and Tariffs (GATT), the World Trade Organization (WTO), and the North American Free Trade Agreement (NAFTA), the MAI was an international bill of rights for transnational corporations. The intent was to reduce restrictions on investment in production and thereby increase the freedom of the labor, environmental, and social practices of investors (read corporations).

The attempt at an agreement was a reaction to growing resistance by governments, grass-roots organizations, and communities, particularly in poorer countries, who are becoming aware of the power wielded by these corporations and the danger to life and limb that they present. The MAI would have prevented local governments from stating regulatory claims in their own territories, and would have subjected protesting states to penalties ranging from removal from Most Favored Nation Status to severe financial fines and forfeiture.

Not to be easily defeated, the negotiators of the agreement, spearheaded by the twenty-nine industrialized countries of the Organization for Economic Cooperation and Development (OECD), are gearing up to pass similar measures through the WTO. These multilateral organizations exist, of course, to facilitate the increasing globalization of the economy, affecting labor practices both at home and abroad as the search for cheap labor and increased profit dominate managerial planning.

The December 1999 WTO meeting in Seattle was similarly greeted with mass protests against secret negotiations that would destroy the sovereignty of nations and further compromise labor standards, the environment, and the ability of peoples around the globe to have a say in their own reproduction. While some of the strategies and tactics of this well-organized opposition can be questioned, it was the first time mass demonstrations against the multinational organization of corporations and the effects of these organizations on local areas had taken place in the United States. The activity of these organizations, both for and against, is overtly political: their strategies are implemented to gain or lessen further access to resources that will increase profit and accumulation. They have a goal in mind.

Against this backdrop, the use of *"queer" as politic has a terrifyingly ambiguous status*. It represents an opposition that does not oppose. It includes the spectrum of ideologies from left to right, with the caveat that the *theory* generated around it is primarily neo-conservative, suggesting that the organizing of collective action is all but impossible.

Legitimization in Queer theory means the right to be just as one is, a kind of free activity that incorporates gender, sexuality, and individual variants in thought and speech. The problem, of course, lies in the fact that this process of legitimization does not create equality: dominance still exists, ideals still rule the day. But legitimization is not only "the right to be." According to Epstein,

> I take it as a given that power inheres in the ability to name, and what we call ourselves has implications for political practice. An additional assumption is that lesbians and gay men in our society consciously seek, in a wide variety of ways, to *legitimate* their forms of sexual expression, by developing explanations, strategies and defenses. These legitimations are articulated both on an individual level ("this is who I am, and this is why I'm that way") and on a collective level ("This is what we are, and here is what we should do"). Legitimation strategies play a mediating function between self-understanding and political programs, and between groups and their individual members.
>
> (Epstein, 1987: 23)

The key phrase here is "what we should do." The problem we encounter with Queer theory is that the collective level is deemed impossible: the legitimating function is purely personal, the ultimate statement of "the personal as political." Indeed, when Judith Butler was asked for suggestions on how to proceed in the political arena, she answered:

> I actually believe that politics has a character of contingency and context to it that cannot be predicted at the level of theory. And that when theory starts becoming programmatic, such as "here are my five prescriptions", and I set up my typology, and my final chapter is called "What is to be Done?", it preempts the whole problem of context and contingency, and I do think that political decisions are made in that lived moment and they can't be predicted

from the level of theory – they can be sketched, they can be prepared for but I suppose I'm with Foucault on this … It seems like a noble tradition.

(Bell, 1999: 167)

But context and contingency, and the "lived moment," are aspects of personal recognition, and a failure to specify leads nowhere. Simple reflection on the success of *movements* around the world and throughout modern history tells us otherwise.

If our goal is to produce a society that accepts difference, welcomes diversity, and champions human rights, how do we get there? Working towards structural change requires strategies for social change, which is what answering the question "what is to be done" entails. We can learn from past successes and analytical mistakes. Just as Oscar Lewis's (1963) belief that the "culture of poverty" could only be broken through intensive psychotherapy ignored the structures that created it, so we too must recognize that the conditions of oppression are not self-generated. Anything else is blaming the victim.

## *Identifying with* social movements

The overcoming of obstacles is in itself a liberating activity.

(Marx, 1973: 611)

Without a revolutionary theory there can be no revolutionary movement.

(Lenin, *What is to be Done?*)

In recent academic literature there is a distinction made between the "new social movements" and those of the "old left." This demarcation reflects the differences between struggles that were rooted in working-class unionism and the fight against overt capitalist control in everyday life, and more recent developments directed at specific areas of interest such as gender, the environment, ethnic recognition, and identity.[1] The "post-industrialist" strategy characteristic of these movements assumes that old class distinctions are being blurred as technology and consumption create divergences emphasizing relative *position* rather than class.

I argued in Chapter 4 that much of the confusion around class is derived from a blurring of status and class. Class is a structural position in relation to capitalist accumulation, while status is achieved through consumption and the perception of power. Yet any discussion of globalization and the internationalization of production, exchange, redistribution, and consumption reveals the speciousness of any claim that we live in a "post-industrialist" world. Industry has not disappeared (for who would produce what we consume?). It has just been transformed. Furthermore, the denial of the reality of class seems preposterous in the face of statistics that document the widening gap between rich and poor, the movement of capital in search of the cheap exploitation of workers, and the strategies that are being produced by managers and owners of capitalist enterprises. Viewing class as real in this way does not mean we have to view it as omnipotent, or as the *only* mode of analysis.

*Identifying with* social movements in an era of global capitalist accumulation presupposes a recognition that exploitation, prejudice, and violence are facts of everyday life; it is not, however, necessary to agree with all of the beliefs of your neighbor to establish a mutually supportive alliance. Nor is it necessary actually to *experience* the reality of your cohorts to identify with common causes. In other words, it is necessary to refocus on practice-unifying and practice-generating principles (Bourdieu, 1982: 101).[2] The ability to create a true political movement assumes an identification with the struggles and projected outcomes of that movement while recognizing the differences between the movement's members that need to be accommodated. The process is liberatory. The characters that Duberman documents in his exposition of Stonewall (1993) all differ in their backgrounds and in their understanding of the world at large. The movement generated by Stonewall cut across class and status, but its general demands were the same for all: an end to discrimination and persecution.

Castells' (1997) notion of project identity is again helpful here in defining the parameters of social movements. The movements for colonial independence were specifically geared towards the rights of indigenous peoples and gaining freedom from exploitation. The anti-war movement, however much divisiveness it generated, was still focused on the right to self-determination for the Vietnamese. Past feminist struggles, despite incidents that threatened to destroy basic alliances, pulled together women of differing class, status, race, and sexual orientation. While it has not always been possible for these segments to productively work with each other, there has at least been a common understanding of the goals of liberation.

The recognition of common goals can give rise to an identification based on common purpose. One need not have the same sexual orientation or the same taste in fashion to understand that discrimination exists and therefore to embark on a fight against it together. Yet one example of the most striking divisions in the queer movement – that between gay men and lesbians – remains. This separation is most evident in the social arena, though it has also driven wedges between gays and lesbians in the political realm. This is more than a product of natural affiliation: it illustrates the general mode of operation of a capitalist hegemony, which seeks to create divisions in order to maintain control. Furthermore, those oppressed by both race and gender find themselves at odds with both white gay men and lesbians. Transgendered and transsexual individuals feel marginalized within the queer movement as a whole, while working-class gay men and lesbians are often shut out of the discussion altogether.[3] Lesbians and gay men, as Weeks (1985) recognizes, are not two genders within one sexual category. They have histories that are differentiated, because of the complex organization of male and female identities, precisely along lines of gender. But in a culture where homosexual desires are not fully accepted, those identities constitute a precondition for political action:

> To argue that "anything goes" is to fall back into an easy libertarianism which ignores questions of power and the quality of relationships … There exists a plurality of sexual desires, of potential ways of life, and of relationships. A radical sexual politics affirms a freedom to be able to choose between them … Identity may, in the end, be no more than a game, a ploy to enjoy particular types of relationships and pleasures. But without it, it seems, the possibilities of sexual choice are not increased but diminished. The recognition of "sexual identities," in all their ambivalence, seems to be the precondition for the realization of sexual diversity.
>
> (Weeks, 1985: 210)

Hennessy (1994) reasons that true incorporation would entail more than the granting of civil rights: "It also requires eliminating the inequities between the haves and the have-nots that allows tolerance of 'minorities' necessary" (1994: 89). The focus on local, specific realities supports a negation of the discussion of larger systemic issues, the "grand narratives" that the postmodernists would have us dismiss. This leaves politics in the realm of narrowly defined causes, a strategy that Nancy Fraser and Linda Nicholson would seem to support by describing "mature" feminist theory as focusing on "more concrete inquiry with more limited aims" rather than on the larger issues of, say, "gender identity" (Fraser and Nicholson, 1989: 98). This assertion points both to the relativist position of its purveyors and to a consistent misreading of a materialist perspective that has become commonplace. For as O'Laughlin suggested much earlier, "such a solution is only possible if we have a general theory through which to analyze the ways that cultural representations are socially organized and reproduced" (1975: 348). While these sorts of neo-liberal constructions of social thought, which maintain the necessity for liberty, fraternity, and equality for all, are well-intentioned, there still exists on the part of many academics, in Carol Vance's words, "a reluctance to lose privileges attendant upon their being members of the majority and a fear of losing their claims to political savvy if they do not side with the newly vocal, emerging minorities" (Hennessy, 1994: 93). This is an aspect of the "personal as political" often ignored in the rush to generate theory. The theorists themselves, consciously or not, may see themselves as having much to lose if their heightened position is devalued in favor of a more radicalized reckoning of class. The fact, as Hennessy notices, that any analysis of capitalism is notoriously absent from new social criticism in the postmodernist mode is reason enough to view it with a critical eye. Reflecting on his own participation in gay and lesbian politics, Duberman noticed that,

Working within the system had, I acknowledged, produced some important gains; we *had*, overall, achieved greater visibility and more legal protection. But the gains had come at no small cost: We had taken to downplaying our differences from the mainstream ...

It is true that political involvement requires some detachment from self-obsession. But ... [p]articipation in common struggle with others opens up opportunities that feed the self in unexpected ways. Though political work *does* demand that we concentrate on the public purpose at hand, it simultaneously provides the individual with the comfort of community and newfound security and confidence.

(Duberman, 1996: 89)

Lacking other models, the early homophile movements were founded by individuals who took the tenets of the Communist Party as their basis for organization, the Stalinist bases of which frequently de-emphasized the importance of inclusion as central to organization.[4] This clearly unacceptable stance has been confused by the purveyors of the new theory with a truly materialist interpretation of the phenomenon of the oppressed, of their place in the wider context of the culture, and of the fight for "minority" rights. Looked at this way, the study of culture becomes essential. The ways in which reaction, oppression, and discrimination are worked out on the ground are essential to an understanding of the survival of the system that produces them.

Within the queer movement, then, clashes among segments claiming specific interests have produced inevitable schisms. In the sense that Queer theorists have worked toward transcending these differences by urging their deconstruction, their project can be viewed as a commendable attempt at derailing these conflicts through designification. But it does not confront the very real issues that remain.

## The appropriation of energy

Capitalist production and its relations of work and social life appropriate energy, both natural and social, and organize it in a particular way. The struggle to maintain the energy necessary to counter the forces of exploitation and oppression is present in all social movements. Relatively recent history presents the experiences of both the AIDS and the anti-war movements as examples of struggles that needed to be continually regenerated to move forward. The current passivity being evidenced in the fight against AIDS, both domestically and internationally, attests to the power of dominant ideologies in shaping the progression of these movements.

The capture of energy for the organization of opposition movements invariably must confront the problem of dominant structures that work to usurp the resources needed to sustain collective action. As both Marx and Freud suggested, the suppression of self-actualization that is experienced as both oppression and repression produces tensions. Such tensions are being witnessed in the current queer movement as oppositional politics: a politics based on difference. These very real contradictions are sometimes manageable and sometimes not.[5] Queer theory has incorporated these oppositions as articles of primary analysis without including an account of the organization of energy by the purveyors of power.

In the 1940s, the American anthropologist Leslie White argued that energy is commonly invoked to explain processes of technological and physical change and it is justifiably applied to social organization. Organization, he argued, is a kind of technology, using mental energy to accomplish the tasks of social structure.[6] The division of labor is a facet of the intersection of human energy and the environment, the result of which is the creation of culture.[7] Culture is a mechanism for harnessing energy, both physical and mental, he argued, adding the important caveat that "energy has to be put to work" (1949: 348). Advance in cultural development, it follows, is a consequence of the amount of energy controlled and used, and further advance is predicated on the ways in which people as social beings are able to redirect and harness new forms of energy. Here, as in the physical world, energy is "neither created nor annihilated, at least not within cultural systems; it is merely transformed" (1949: 374). This process is mediated by institutional systems of control that function to coordinate various parts of the social system into a coherent whole. In class societies, those who control this energy are those in positions of power. As V. Gordon Childe suggested, "the social system operates not only to concentrate wealth in the hands of the ruling minority but effectively prevent[s] the fruits of the technological process from being distributed among the masses of the population" (White, 1949: 383).

The redirection of energy toward political ends is a power struggle that involves every aspect of social reproduction. Multinational organizations have taken the lead in the organization of energy, physical and social, to meet the needs of capital accumulation. They have quickly succeeded in reorganizing production, weakening labor movements, and destroying communities. The insecurity among populations that occurs when daily needs are not met is then preferably explained by concrete, quickly understandable, and readily provided means by those generating ideology. The result is the scapegoating of groups and populations that are perceived as responsible for the downturn in people's ability to provide for themselves. By contrast with the immediacy of the resources obtained when corporations seek out and exploit new forms of labor – whether immigrants, new populations or robots – resistance movements also need to *create* their energy to counter imposed structures. At this point in capitalist development, can sufficient social force be generated to direct existing energy towards the production of movements that further human rights and justice? Can the energy that the owners and organizers of capital are so adept at appropriating be usurped to place human needs before the needs of accumulation? States have become increasingly sophisticated at convincing citizens that they are acting in their best interests. This often works against an inherent, local knowledge that comes with the experience of everyday activity, and produces a noted resignation, an apathy that approaches social depression, visible among the populations of, at least, the advanced capitalist countries. What can we identify as similar energetic patterns of exploitation? Finally, can the energy feeding these maladaptive responses be redirected towards the creation of social movements and the call to end inequality?

We know that in capitalist societies those in power are in control over the means and rewards of production. They are the same individuals and classes that effect the production of what we call the *dominant* culture, the nexus of relationships and ideas that condition the way that individual members of the society act in accordance with the rules and structure that govern social functioning. While White overstated his case when he claimed that the individual has no place in the science of culture, he called forth the important debate about the role of the individual in culture and society that is at the forefront of the debates in Queer theory and its antecedents.[8] The relationships between the individual and society, between the personal and the political, are central grappling points.

The personal becomes political when we can integrate the individual into society and look for modes of social life, including social involvement and action, that include both. This necessarily involves analyses that embody psychoanalytic and social theory. As one example, Brennan (1993) incorporates a concept of energy into psychoanalytic theory encompassing the effect of exploitation and oppression on the individual, and the individual's response to these social phenomena. For Brennan, the ego needs "fixed points" to focus its identification with others and to understand its position within society. Through these points the individual becomes a social actor with a sense of uniqueness and purpose. But for the present, the ego exists within the confines of capitalist society, and capitalism operates through the production of commodities. These commodities

> block the mobility of psychic energy; the technologically fixed points of commodities, unless they are constructed with care, block the regeneration of nature and natural energy ... In an interactive understanding of energy, the barriers that we erect between thought and matter, individual and environment, are precisely socially constructed ones. What happens on the socially constructed outside has energetic consequences for the psyche.
>
> (Brennan, 1993: xii)[9]

In a fashion similar to the other theorists discussed in the present work, Brennan traces the "idea of the contained individual," reminding us that not all cultures see the individual as indivisible and autonomous. Individuality is an integral part of the "ego's era," a Western event, historically and culturally specific (1993: 83). On the level of energy, then, exploitation is both personal and political, for the "contained subject" maintains individuality by defending oneself and finding blame for personal anxieties in other individuals and groups.

In this way, individualism is energy harnessed in a particular form, substituting for other forms that have historically appeared. Moreover, since exploitation always involves a transfer of energy, the results of that transfer condition the culture and appear to organize it. In Brennan's words,

> exploitation in these terms does not only work on the economic level. It works at the interpersonal level as well, the level experienced in everyday personal and social life. In personal life, the wrong sex can assign one to a draining emotional tie, and an inexplicable fixity or inertia. In social interaction, this exploitation may be brief or glancing, but it is pervasive: the wrong accent, the wrong colour, the wrong sexuality can lead to a thousand slights in brief encounters, all of which give a temporary leverage to the subjects on the other side of them.
>
> (Brennan, 1993: 185)

Thus, the straight man or woman may "fix" his or her own anxieties about the ideals of sexuality onto queers. Similarly, the white man or woman may "fix" similar anxieties, especially anxieties about meeting a proposed ideal regarding "success," onto those of a different color or ethnicity, in an attempt to free up his or her own self-confidence at the expense of the other's self-respect. However, the appearance should not be construed alone as a causal sequence, for culture is not organized by inter-subjective relationships alone. The individual and the social levels reinforce each other. The economic structure of exploitation is repeated in microcosm on the personal level. In a capitalist world, built on exploitations of energies, be it economic or intra-psychic, people suffering exploitation based on race, gender, or sexual orientation have fewer energy resources to work against both their own social and personal "fixing," and the consequences of the "fixing" of others onto them. What queers have in common with all others in oppressed positions is this social structure of interpersonal exploitation that creates the conditions for being the receptacles of anxiety transfer and for the carrying of negative affects for those with the power to exploit others. Who these "others" are, whether stigmatized by sexual orientation, race, gender, ethnicity, or other "differences," can vary. Those who are subject to the "fixing" of those in dominant positions are subject to the experience of the tactics of their oppressors, and can mistakenly attempt to do the same, as can be seen in the present personal conflicts that are deceptively based on racial and ethnic conflict but are in fact created by the lack of access to life-sustaining resources around the world, as well as in the conflicts seen within movements of the oppressed. This carrying of oppositional feelings enforces the general structure of economic exploitation.

Rather than create divisions, the lack of access to the broader culture experienced by those who are exploited can also be the basis of attempts to establish alliances through social action and social movements. The task for those who recognize exploitation or are in movements of resistance, then, is to recognize the common connections and areas of exploitation, both economic and intra-psychic, between us – the common connections that work for both good and ill, in the functioning and fabric of our situated lives. Social movements rely on the energy of individuals and groups to organize, lead, and continue activities. Movements for social justice, recognition, and institutional change require sustained, directed, and intensive energy as they act to subvert and resist well-maintained modes of domination.

## Resistance movements

The first movement organized around homosexuality took place in late nineteenth-century Germany (cf. Adam, 1995). This period, of course, does not demarcate the origin of same-sex relationships but the first time the *category* of homosexuals was demarcated in social struggle. It corresponds with the time that the label "homosexual" was used to name individuals in a labeled practice. The categorization coincided with the full-blown genesis of capitalism, and in turn produced movements to defend the right of homosexuals to exist.[10]

The present designation of "queer" is a position that reflects both a history of resistance against oppression and current social conditions. The homophile movement acted in the context of a social sphere that was conservative and reactionary with regard to sex and gender. The "sexual revolution" of the 1960s and 1970s promoted freedom of experience and created grounds for the wider recognition of inequality, providing the possibilities for mass resistance. Our current period is built on these experiences but it also incorporates neo-conservative trends that have been generated by the world-wide expansion of capital. They are felt in society at large, both in public policy and in academia.

As I mentioned earlier, the homophile movements took as their model of organization a Stalinist view of "minorities" as subjugated groups that needed to be led to revolt. The organizations found their members in the union movements and veterans groups of New York and Los Angeles. These organizations were closely tied to the anti-Korean war movement. The Mattachine Society, a purposefully political organization, recognized that capitalism generated oppression. By 1953, there were over 100 discussion groups in southern California alone.[11] But as both Adam and D'Emilio show, the conservative climate of the 1950s led to a withdrawal of specifically anti-capitalist strategies, culminating in the 1953 Mattachine convention that elected an openly anti-communist coordinating council and set the tone for more than a decade (Adam, 1995: 69). The new direction favored assimilation over the fight for rights, declaring that the more one looked like a mainstream member of society, the more successful one could be. The Daughters of Bilitis, formed in 1955, followed the example of the Mattachine Society, promoting an assimilationist strategy minimizing conflict and expressions of difference.[12] The McCarthy era reinforced the fears of retaliation felt by the members of these groups, and their platforms became increasingly unable to confront directly the growing discrimination of "others," which included racial and ethnic minorities.

The 1960s witnessed a period of reevaluation of past methods in every arena. Buoyed by a growing economy benefiting more Americans than ever before, and with the movements for racial equality providing examples of successful organization, members of the Mattachine Society openly engaged in debate about the necessity of asserting gay rights. In 1964, a new leadership formed that favored the fight for equality over assimilation. These changes were very much in step with other communities fighting for recognition and acceptance: the movements for racial equality grew and became more radical just as the anti-Vietnam War movement was gaining a foothold in the American consciousness. Together they created more organizations and communities that worked toward the expression of silenced voices. Despite the ultimate breakdown of organizations like the Students for a Democratic Society, which had no sustaining leadership, a lasting result of these activities was a growing awareness by peoples the world over that equality was a goal worth fighting for. The subsequent growth of the feminist, gay and lesbian, and queer movements stands as a testament to this period.

The current movements for sexual, gender, and racial equality are closely tied to new concepts of difference, acceptance, and assimilation. Contention within the New Left movements of the earlier period threw into relief the need for an appreciation of the nature of difference and the differing needs and experiences of various groups. A lack of clear vision, coupled with the current social climate that includes the processes of the aforementioned struggles of class, however, has heightened this awareness to a fault. The priority of "awareness" over organization has often rendered calls for collective action impotent. At the same time, capital-intensive corporations have been in the forefront of a world-wide expansion that has changed the character of daily life, ideologically blurring material distinctions in the workplace and providing a real threat to organizations of resistance. As we know, when communities resisted the changes in structural conditions at work, many industries simply moved. This strategy by multinationals continues as technology has enabled a freedom of transfer, and as government-backed strategies for trade and investment that attempt to weaken resistance continue to evolve.[13]

The development of queer movements closely follows the history of industry. While multinationals' overseas expansion and their movement into less capital-intensive areas have led to movements for human rights, action toward this goal is often militated against by the fear in communities of the loss of means of subsistence. On a more individual level, it is in a similar way that many fear being "out" in the workplace will cost them their jobs. In the United States, at least, such fear has once again led to a growing tendency towards assimilation within mainstream politics and culture.[14] AIDS organizations have been exceptionally active in generating a radical politics, but a waning of the energy needed to sustain activity, and a conscious propaganda campaign claiming AIDS to be a disease of the past, have also worked against sustained organization. Likewise, the debates around difference and an antagonism to organization in groups like Queer Nation sapped their energy and ultimately led to their destruction.

Organizations like the Human Rights Campaign, lobbying for rights as it supports mainstream candidates, persistently promote queer rights within a culturally acceptable narrow framework. A recent statement that the Campaign supported over 85 per cent of winning candidates belies the contradiction inherent in this kind of politics. The obvious question is, if this is the case, why do Congress, the Senate, and state governments remain so homophobic? Who is represented by this supposedly progressive 85 per cent?[15]

The strategies that can invoke real change are therefore thrown into question. Repeated experience has shown us that working within mainstream politics runs counter to the realities of power: any benefits that are won can be and are quickly revoked as fashions shift and as new opportunities for profit accumulation arise.[16]

Adam (1995) reiterates that gay and lesbian political activity has relied on engaging institutions of the state for the incorporation of queers into civil society in the name of citizenship. In countries that have a history of such incorporation, or where right-wing politics does not have the same influence as it does in the United States, this strategy has, he notes, led to at least a recognition of queer existence (1995: 145). But as he also tells us, many have contested the strict categorization of gay and lesbian that produces a tendency to drive diverse groups of people into mainstreamed acceptance of current politics.

But the problem here is more a product of strategy and leadership than of personal conflict. Had the National Organization of Women, for example, concentrated less on the cultural and experiential aspects of women's identity ("women are different from men") and more on the situated structural position of women – straight, lesbian, bisexual, or otherwise – *while recognizing these cultural differences both inside and outside the movement*, the contentious battles around true recognition may not have functioned so well to work against collective action. The consciousness-raising movement celebrated by more radical early women's movement organizations provided an important forum for women to identify with their peers and to discuss their experiences. But, by design, it did little to challenge the structural bases of power that produced the cultural and social divisions in which women and men are situated. As Adams also correctly points out, the liberal tendency to champion individual sexual practices and beliefs does little to place these individual and social practices in the context of the logic of capitalism, or to reveal the way our representations of male, female, gay, lesbian, and queer have been influenced by it (1995: 152). Instead of directly confronting the aspects of discrimination that are rampant in current relations of work and living, energy has been geared towards the litigation of sexual harassment, the legal age of sexual engagement, and the preserving of individual rights.

The continuing fragmentation of queer politics has had a direct effect on our ability to organize around issues that are not presented by mainstream organizations. Mainstream politics becomes the only viable outlet for the expression of discontent as attempts to organize around more basic issues of oppression involute into interminable discussions of cultural politics. Thus Judith Butler states:

> The critical task for feminism is not to establish a point of view outside of constructed identities; that conceit is the construction of an epistemological model that would disavow its own cultural location and, hence, promote itself as a global subject, a position that deploys precisely the imperialist strategies of subversive repetition enabled by those constructions, to affirm the local possibilities of intervention through participating in precisely those practices of repetition that constitute identity and, therefore, present the immanent possibility of contesting them.
>
> (Butler, 1990: 147)

My argument throughout this work is that these remarks, which reflect a general mode of inquiry, are both incomprehensible and misguided. They subsume the socially constructed identity of individuals under a rubric of opportunism, ignoring the real epistemology of social construction that includes a real political economy of reproduction.

## Class, race, gender, and social resistance

As individuals, we all wrestle with modes of social power that influence how we see ourselves and, in turn, influence our ability to react, defend, and assert ourselves. Whether we identify as workers, gays and lesbians, queers, colonial subjects, or racial minorities, there is a commonality in the way in which capitalism invokes these categories to maintain ideological hegemony. But recognizing the ideological means through which categorization and oppression operate does not negate the material foundations of their development. The ideological realm cannot be changed unless the energetic as well as the economic basis for its generation is challenged and defeated.

With these ideas we must return to a basic understanding of the root of exploitation, the misuse of the environment, the abuse of labor, and the genesis of sexual and gender oppression. For, despite views to the contrary, we are still dealing with class oppositions today just as we were at the beginning of capitalism, and during the development of the "old" social movements. The facts of exploitation and the means by which basic human needs are met have not changed all that much, though the forms taken by these processes have significantly evolved. Human consciousness is itself realized, as Martyn Lee comments, "objectified in the material products of labor ... that is why the object of labor – the material artifact – holds a central space in the determination of the ontological health of individuals and society in general" (1992: 43). Which is to say that there is a reality, found in the labor process and other social relations, to the reproduction of self and others that cannot be reduced to language. A politics that assumes social change must be oriented toward a confrontation with the very nature of the social structure. Labor, as *sensuous activity*, is a human phenomenon; it encompasses both the means by which we create ourselves and the ways in which we experience the world.

*Identifying with* social movements on the basis of similar patterns of exploitation, rather than mechanistically deconstructing them, can begin to resolve the stagnation that has dominated attempts to develop coalitions around issues that matter.

A truly radicalized politics assumes that the goal of analysis *and* action is the transformation of a culture that diminishes freedom and choice. Any movement that claims to work toward eliminating these culturally rooted elements of the dominant ideology must recognize that constructions of gender and sexuality are connected to the maintenance of the social order. Asserting the centrality of gender and sexuality in public life, while challenging the economic and political relationships that sustain discrimination is the only path to ensuring success. Struggling for acceptance within mainstream politics mistakes influence for real power, enlarging an ill-conceived hope that working within the structures that create oppression can change them.[17] Even those who agree with the basic tenets of capitalism (and I refer here to organizations like the gay Log Cabin sector of the Republican Party) inherently misinterpret the workings of power if power is understood in energetic rather than Foucaultian terms. By way of illustration, we need only to remember that the AIDS movement started as a white, middle-class, male phenomenon, and while many AIDS service organizations have since attempted to broaden their perspective to include other sectors of a diverse population, the lack of larger purpose has led to fragmentation within these organizations. Such myopia has also led to an almost complete dismissal of AIDS as a problem. With the advent of new drugs that many cannot tolerate or afford, and that do not promise long-term success, we have heard statements from "leaders" such as Andrew Sullivan, the former editor of *The New Republic*, claiming that the AIDS crisis has ended. This complete lack of perspective on how AIDS has affected less privileged populations (not to mention populations around the world) has ultimately caved in on itself. There is less funding for AIDS research being generated by federal, state, and local governments, and less activism promoted by those who have benefited most by new technologies. Technology, of course, is produced for profit, and small gains produce big rewards for pharmaceutical companies. The media campaign that has declared the AIDS problem solved as long as those infected keep taking their drugs is but another vehicle for downplaying the seriousness of the crisis and the social structure that first produced and then, in turn, ignored it. But as the infection rate rises around the globe, particularly among a younger generation, and as the promise of these new pharmaceutical technologies is shown less successful than hoped, this position becomes more and more untenable.

Here we assert again that the dismissal of a class analysis in a global system dominated by capital can only lead to disappointments and setbacks, especially in understanding the energetic nature of class exploitation and helping us link it to the exploitation of other groups. Likewise, discussions which foreground a gender analysis around, for example, biological boundaries and the role of childbearing in establishing the roots of subjugation, have little consequence on the mechanisms of domination that exist in very real time. The self-declared "queer movement" has largely been a "middle-class" phenomenon concentrating on gaining the same rights as "middle-class" heterosexuals within society. But despite the differences in the oppression of women, queers, and racial minorities, there are real connections that unite these groups both economically and energetically in the political domain.

# Conclusion

## Theory, politics, and the community

In communities we identify, support, and build connections, geographic and emotional, with each other. Communities act to connect individuals with the social. They provide the avenues for human social reproduction and serve as the basis for mutual support. Moreover, communities can be sanctuaries for people needing to recover from oppression, and they can provide for collective strategies against those who attempt to destroy and subjugate their members.

Marx identified the three sources of alienation in capitalist society, June Nash tells us, as:

> (1) the separation of producers from the product, or the alienation of surplus value; (2) separation of producers from the means of production, which forces them to become dependent on the owners of capital to make a living; and (3) separation of the producers from the source of meaningful self-involvement in the work process.
>
> (Nash, 1979: 325)

To this Nash adds a fourth component: "the separation of the worker from the sense of identity with a community" (1979: 325). The separation of community members from each other, or the destruction of the energetic relations of community, is a fifth component.

Whether these facets of alienation are seen as structurally imposed or psychologically based, the alienated individual cannot summon the energy needed to connect functionally or to alter structures of power in such a way that makes it possible to express one's full potential. This is only possible when there is adequate support for doing so.

In the present work, I have offered an extended discussion of the effects of capitalism on the development of theory. This is not an academic exercise. The history of capitalist development has shown it to be structurally antagonistic to the healthy maintenance of community and identity, however the latter is conceived. There is no easy sustenance of community under capitalist relations of production. The control of capital is a function of structural power which enables the generation of wealth. Herein lies the essential truth of a society based on the uneven distribution of resources: it produces owners of production and the rewards of labor, and it produces those who work for them – it creates classes. All the blurring that takes place in-between is in the province of what anthropologists call "complex society," which refers to the many ways in which social organization in multi-faceted systems generates avenues of social reproduction. The truth remains that demands of class hegemony in capitalism produce inequality, discrimination, war, and genocide.

We know that classes are not mutually exclusive entities that exist in time and space without conflict. The tension that the struggle over the control of production creates is central to daily living. Through this struggle, ideology is created to lessen the appearance of exploitation and subjugation. As a means of creating "ideas in the service of power," as Therborn (1980) put it, the managers of capitalism offset the appearance of attempts at control.

The participants in this process rationalize dominant modes of ideology that support the current social structure. These ideologies, seen in academic circles in the form of theories, can be contested and resisted, but their power to influence and to set the standards for discussion cannot be dismissed.

From the early enclosure movement in England, which separated communities from their lands, to the incursions of imperialism and colonialism that destroyed communities and/or grouped them into "tribes," and to the neo-colonialist mechanisms of globalization, the owners of capital seek their own advantage. The development of the global economy is a product of, and represents a furtherance of, these goals. Capitalist enterprises are no longer confronted with the drag of local initiatives and concerns. Trade agreements and legislated specifications on multilateral investment are attempts to subjugate without the overt use of force. What we now witness is a generalized instability that produces famine, racism, ethnic conflict, and the rise of nationalist ideology, with the presence and threat of catastrophic war a constant feature of global dynamics.

My argument has been that the development of theory which takes the idea of the self-contained individual for granted is a part of this process of class struggle. Postmodernism and post-structuralism, as examples of academic theory that reifies the self, serve the *goals* of the capitalist enterprise by promoting the isolation of the individual and the fragmentation of resistance. Fragmentation and isolation are strategies of capitalist management. These strategies would have the owners of capital in charge of thought and action. Resistance to capitalist managerial tactics is embedded in class struggle, which is dependent on identification, both energetically and economically, and the communities that support the identification process.

Queer theory, as currently focused, is embedded in the context of class oppositions, and, paradoxically, the consequences of the theory are not what it appears to avow or what it contends it is. Instead of a force that opposes the dominance of power by those that control capital, it works as a part of the ideological mechanism that those in power seek to further. With the language of past radical movements, Queer theory works against the struggle it claims to engage, and as reified self-involvement it militates against the construction and building of communities. It disengages the energetic level of alliances and interpersonal relations, only to refocus efforts on the reductionistic deconstruction of texts interpreted only for personal use.

The presence of conflict among peoples is tied to the struggle to maintain community and identity. What presents as senseless bigotry, sometimes resulting in genocide, is rooted in the anxious fight to maintain families, communities, and ensure survival. These are not individual functions. Their strategies, misconceived and misdirected, are a direct consequence of the loss of self-empowerment and control over everyday life. Capitalism, in this way, gives rise to psychological as well as social consequences.

When communities are weakened or destroyed, reactions inevitably occur at the individual level. No longer connected to the stability of the group where there is mutual support and no longer ensured of a future at all, individuals suffer. There is now an epidemic of suicide, depression, and violence in Western cultures. The recent spate of killings in high schools in the United States is one tragic manifestation of this kind of alienation, of the inability to connect and to identify with others. It is the failure of what present populist ideology would have us believe is the failure of "family values." Indeed this is true. But the genesis of this destruction is not to be found in the misdeeds of parents and psychotics, but in the structural disassembling of the means to make and affirm concrete connections.

Yet despite these forceful attempts at destroying the means by which people interact with each other, the effort to maintain and build communities remains. Whether fought in a geographic location or by means of gender, racial, or class identifications, the struggles continue. The structures of energetic power that enforce capitalist production have not succeeded in destroying the processes of identification. They have even, as we have seen, provided the means to further them. Communities around the world, whether they be on the Mexican border, the jungles of South America or the cities of the United States, are generating new forms of organization that possess the possibility of real resistance against the mechanisms of alienation, fragmentation, and destruction. The necessary task in the application of organization and social theory is to recognize the importance of furthering these developments, and of *identifying with* them.

## The queer community

Communities within queer movements have become increasingly fragmented, and the impetus for resistance has been consequently weakened. The lesbian community is beset with problems regarding differences in labeling and focus, while the gay male community is barraged with obsessive messages regarding status and consumption. The queer community is traversed by concepts of difference. These differences have been reinforced by the postmodernist and post-structuralist turn, which has separated individuals into incomparable units and, as I emphasize, tacitly idealized the goals of late capitalism.

Lesbian, gay, bisexual, and transgendered/transsexual are categories that represent differing needs and positions within our present culture but which have a common heritage. Despite their different placement in the context of social experience, they also have in common the generalized forms of exploitation that occur along racial, ethnic, and class lines. Indeed, as I and many others have documented, it was the movements that grew out of the resistance to capitalist forms of domination and power that brought about the genesis of queer movements and gave us the means for the recognition of common goals. The distinctions among these various identifications result from lived experience *and* from the general course of separation and alienation that is evidenced in late capitalism. Backed by the ideology of postmodernist principles, the individual (or non-individual as the case may have it) becomes a receptacle of culture and desire. As Eagleton has edgily remarked,

> Much postmodernism has sprung from the United States, or at least has taken rapid root there, and reflects some of that country's most intractable political problems. It is then perhaps a little ethnocentric of this anti-ethnocentrism, though hardly a gesture unknown to that nation, to project its own political backyard onto the world at large. There is now an institute for postmodern studies at the University of Beijing, as China imports Derrida along with Diet Coke. If postmodernism is a form of culturalism, it is be-cause among other reasons it refuses to recognize that what different ethnic groups have in common socially and economically is finally more important that their cultural differences. More important for what? For the purposes of their political emancipation.
>
> (Eagleton, 1997: 122)

We could add here that, even if they are not stigmatized in a particular economic group, they too share in the energetic exploitation of all those who are the focus of manipulated labeling. But the final question is, how can we bypass these forces of disintegration? How do we unite against them?

## Queer communities as part-cultures

To the extent that many in queer studies separate out what is "queer" from the larger culture, they insist that resistance to dominant modes of thought is best approached by dismissing the power of the dominant ideology. There is often an allied refusal on the part of queer writers to include heterosexuality as a baseline for discussion. The claim is that the focus on heterosexual relations necessarily positions any contrary affirmation of sexuality and gender as an "other," rather than as a positive site of inquiry in itself. By ruling out the dominant discourse, many argue, an alternative culture can be formed, one that does not include or exclude but exists by right in its own location. But we then ignore the fact that we live our daily lives in relation to the mode of work and reproduction around us. Attempting to ignore the power and ideology that creates the basis for daily functioning affronts the activity that engenders experience: queer individuals buy houses, rent apartments, drive cars, go to supermarkets, and earn wages for a living; some fight for the right to marry while others demand to be part of the military. This all takes place in a culture where heterosexuality is the norm and capitalist relations of power are predominant.

By posing *part-cultures* as a basis for qualification, we can allow for a more specific rendering of the associative independence of queer individuals and communities vis-á-vis the larger social structure, including social class.[1] That is, while queer communities can act as relatively autonomous domains within larger social formations, they are still part of the larger social structure in which they function. Part-cultures comprise those norms and behaviors that are specific to groupings that hold beliefs and practices significantly differing from the ideology of the dominant culture. They form communities and direct energy to further their own ends, energy that is all the more effective because of solidarity. This sustains not only resistance but an affectional community, in the full sense that we can give to Weeks's (1985) term. While members of gay, lesbian, bisexual, transgendered, and queer communities may attempt to structure their individual lives primarily in relation to each other, a need persists to balance these networks with the demands of the outside world in order to secure the means for daily living. Queer communities are largely urban phenomena, as Seidman (1997) and Clare (1998) recognize, buttressing other communities and inherently tied to and integrated with larger communities. While they may have modes of interaction and beliefs that are specific, to take them as units of analysis in themselves distorts the epistemology of their development.

## Developing strategy

Strategy in this context consists of the ways in which we organize energy to meet the ends we seek to achieve. Strategy as such is the mechanism by which true politics is generated, both on the personal and the political level. A true resistance politics has to incorporate both the micro and the macro levels of analysis to mediate differences and to confront effectively the forces of well-organized opposition.

Lesbian, gay, and queer movements have, so far, depended on the involvement of individuals as the primary drivers of social action. Yet we know from the experience of past movements for social change (and particularly the experience of labor movements) that individuals need to have structural representation in order to maintain the energy needed for sustained opposition. Individuals working against their oppressors, whether in the workplace or neighborhood, cannot succeed without a mechanism that can play a larger role in incorporating them into communities of resistance where mutual recognition is present.

"We're Queer and We're Here" is a necessary declaration of identity. But it is only a moment. Required is a strategy that can institutionalize a movement towards resistance so that change may be recognized as a social necessity. Differences will continue to exist. Black women face the sexism inherent in their relations with men while confronting racism; lesbians are confronted with the hierarchy of sexual politics while dealing with arguments around pornography and sexual pleasure. And more economic issues such as the pervasive and growing feminization of poverty. Bisexual, transsexual, and transgendered peoples are often ignored by all. Queers, in general, encounter the real differences based on status and class as they experience the oppression of the dominant culture. But these are all in fact part of a larger class struggle which is borne out in the conflict of the uses and control of energy and, ultimately, human regeneration. They need to be recognized as such.

The test of a successful movement will be whether we might honor all these divergent interests and experiences, while joining together to forge a successful attempt to redistribute the rewards of labor and to end the violence of prejudice. Resistance, then, involves more than language-based opposition to noxious forces. Real opposition takes place in the realm of reproduction of community and the larger social sphere, on the basis of daily existence and in the realm of social and productive power.

## The promise of civil society

Given the statistics on the increasing power of multinational organizations and managers of capitalist production, the clear gains by multinational organizations that usurp the participation of local economies and movements of resistance, and the focus, by many, on the past failings of the left, an increasingly apocalyptic view of our future has emerged. This view is also reflected in the direction that Queer theory has taken. What can be easily forgotten is the historical role of civil society in countering these structures of oppression, and the ability of peoples around the world to counter daily subjugation.[2]

The recent demonstrations protesting the policies of the World Trade Organization in Seattle and the International Monetary Fund in Washington D.C. speak of a level of commitment that has not been present, in the United States, since the 1960s. Of significant consequence was the organized presence of unions, many of the members of which recognized the importance of sustained organization against the attack on entitlements and rights around the globe. What we are presently witnessing is the building of a social movement unionism, which has the possibilities of overcoming the inherent instabilities of "new social movements" that, while objectively committed to social reform or even social transformation, are easily co-opted into mainstream politics or compromised into positions of questionable tactics.

As Gay Seidman (1994) defines it, social movement unionism is the "effort to raise the living standards of the working class as a whole, rather than to protect individually the defined interests of union members" (1994: 2). Specific union interests have been easily undermined by managerial deals with union leaders and by threats to simply cease production. The ability to defeat these specific interests has resulted in the decreasing power of unionism and of interest in union activity. The current increase in union involvement in the larger issues of community sustainability, human rights, and the push for inclusiveness signal hope for a regeneration. As Moody (1997) puts it in his example of racial groups within Detroit's divided neighborhoods,

> One of the objects of social-movement unionism must be to overcome the spatial separation of different racial groups within the working class through active forms of class struggle, but also by taking to heart the specific needs and demands of communities of color, whether they are "native" or immigrant. What is involved here is neither some liberal notion of racial harmony and integration that must precede class unity, nor some postmodernist or corporate romanticization or diversity which leaves inequality for the vast majority intact, but a more dialectical notion of a fight for equality linked to a fight for class advancement. The movement must learn to draw on all its strengths, of which ethnic concentrations are often one ...
>
> (Moody, 1997: 173)

Brecher *et al.* (2000) note that Seattle marked a turning point in public awareness of global institutions as threats to our very existence. These protests marked globalization broadly, in terms of issues not only of trade but also of community maintenance and reproduction. The significant presence of unions at other demonstrations marked a sea change in the way that unions do "business," both locally and globally.

With an increasing awareness of the necessity of inclusion and the struggle for alliances, unions have also begun to organize sectors of the labor force outside the traditional industrial sector. Service industries – that growing sector of the workforce in capital-intensive countries that are outside the formal industrial sphere – are also being targeted for inclusion in the politics of resistance. While there is recognition that industrial organization must still be a baseline for tactics of resistance, there now also exists the possibility that broader alliances can reinforce these movements, *and* broaden the struggle to include the daily necessities needed for reproduction.

Thus, the labor movement has begun to confront these issues as the character of labor itself has changed. The contributors to *A New Labor Movement for a New Century* (ed. Mantsios, 1998) address the problems that have worked against the creation of a real labor party that would include women, people of color, and queers. Such a party must be forged with an eye to inclusion, and with the realization that inclusion and inequality are more than ever before *international* problems. Social movements in the United States and western Europe cannot isolate themselves at the expense of those in the less capital-intensive nations. Capitalist domination has become widely scattered, while the effects of this domination have traveled back home in the form of stagnant wages and the breakdown of communities.[3]

We are also witnessing another global development that has begun to have substantial effects on the way capital organizes and maintains control over populations: the increasing rise of indigenous social movements that are challenging the regulatory power of capitalist management over community organization. June Nash suggests that these indigenous movements may provide the vanguard for future global resistance, and she documents her case with a study of the Zapatistas of Chiapas, Mexico, and their drive for autonomy that has been organized in community kitchens and the fields of the jungle.[4] Similarly, Warren (1999) shows the rise of indigenous language revitalization and education among Mayan nationalists in Guatemala, pointing to a level of community regeneration that confronts the global economy at its very core.

Together, these developments present a more optimistic view of the future and the possibilities for change. The need here is to identify with those in similar circumstances to our own, generating the kinds of energy needed to counter the power of present structural conditions.

Creative strategies that can work toward the objective of overcoming all oppression, including queer, need to be continually developed and reassessed. For our present purposes, I offer the following, limited, list of such strategies:

1 forming caucuses within local and transnational corporations that recognize the similarities in the oppression experienced by different groups and which assert rights and privileges;
2 developing industry-specific organizing tactics that can confront multinational organizations as they spread throughout the world;
3 working with the labor movement to insure the diversity of leadership and membership that would lead to real inclusion;

4  democracy in the workplace that would ensure equality of representation and recognition of needs;
5  building union organization by active recruitment of workers whose labor has not traditionally been defined within union standards, including those of the service sector and immigrant workers;
6  struggles over public curriculums to include discussions of diversity, gender, and sexuality;
7  working against the continuing alienation of the individual by supporting identity-based community and the mutual support it represents;
8  actively working against the fragmentation of communities that is effected by an emphasis on individual difference;
9  promoting the theoretical work and leadership that recognizes the logic of capitalism and oppression and the negative consequences of neo-conservative theoretical positioning;
10  the support and organization of struggles for rights and inclusion outside the workplace, in the realm of civil society; and finally,
11  working toward the formation of a labor party that represents existing diversity, uniting local, regional, national, and international workers and citizens, and for common causes and rights.

## Queer theory revisited

I started this work by questioning the place of theory in the struggle for equality. Within this framework, the place of academic theory-building and the development of a Queer theory has been questioned and critiqued. Here I restate what I asserted in Chapter 1: we are living in times that are too volatile, too fraught with danger, to ignore the implications and consequences of academic theory and how it is received. I have ended with a call for community: the entity that is developed through identification and mutual support and that acts as a site of resistance to the sources and management of oppressive power that have delegated minorities to a less equal status.

Queer theory has developed along a path that questions the basic tenets of past resistance movements while championing the right of inclusion. But despite calls for the recognition of diversity, it has done little to further a true inclusiveness that would have the ability to form communities of resistance. Again, this is primarily due to the insistence on the uniqueness of the individual and the relativity of experience. The call made by Queer theory is familiar to those who have participated in resistance movements: the assertion of independence from oppressive authority while claiming the right to envision and create new forms of being. But instead of focusing on the creation of a society that guarantees freedom and expression for all, it has instead focused on the individual as the site of change. Indeed, this fear of connection, as argued in Chapter 5, has real possibilities for generating self-harm. The actions of those with power exert dominance in both conscious and unconscious ways, redirecting energy towards objective oppression and subjective self-hate in the process. While the belief that heterosexuality is the norm is purveyed, violence, both psychological and physical, is enacted on those outside of that projected norm, and experienced by them as being "outside" the facets of daily social life. Beyond making it more difficult to identify with others, such alienation causes a reaction to even the attempt to do so. "The right to be oneself" thus becomes a mechanism for self-protection rather than a call for equality.

Current Queer theory's engagement of this fear and concentration on the deconstruction of identity are results of such a reaction to power, a reductionistic view of the possibilities for change generated by the politics of the 1960s and 1970s. The reaction has taken place most prominently in the academy, where the purveyors of this theory are in positions that pose real danger to those opposing them. They have become the new academic elite, complete with editorships of journals, the power to hire, to decide who publishes, to deny tenure, and the ability to apply pressure with regard to which theory is well received and which disregarded. Let there be no mistake: they do act on their privileges. They are self-protective in much the same way that the managers of capitalist enterprises control the organization of work. It is not in their interest to further communities of dissidence, particularly against themselves.

While Queer theory does not call for the destruction of communities, at least by name, its consequences are the same: communities must be deconstructed to free the individual for self-expression.[5] As the individual becomes the center of analysis in all aspects of social life, and as late capitalism emphasizes individualism on a global scale, resistance theory has closely followed the dominant streams. At best, wishful thinking and the consolidation of position underpins this direction, the hope that the *mind* can reframe the significance of harm while one's job is not threatened. At worst, such a stance is in operative support of current structures of capitalist relations of being.

Community, identity, and self-actualization are indeed complementary. Social and emotional health are promoted by active participation with others in community. The community is where "safe space" is created. Power in numbers has been the call of resistance movements world-wide, from anti-colonial struggles to fights for better working conditions. Such struggles have larger outcomes. The community is a forum for debate for the construction of strategy. Communities exist with varied needs that are part of the complexity of society. It is in communities that social change begins in embryonic form. Separatist movements have proven unproductive as the community becomes isolated and involutes with disagreement. Assimilationist movements cannot work toward sustained social change because there is no confrontation with the basis of oppression. The call for individuality is the most harmful strategy of all, for it separates every person from any concrete sense of identity and collective opposition.

In the fullest sense, we must realize that inequality will not be resolved under capitalism. The rewards of labor and reproduction will remain unevenly distributed, compensating those who do not challenge the bases of inequality while oppressing those with a claim to better rights and resources. This does not mean a retreat into resignation, however. Processes of change are not binary. Working towards change that can challenge the energetic tenets of inequality builds communities that can further the goals of equal participation. Weeks (1985) tells us that the causes of class struggle, feminism, socialism, and gay and lesbian rights all have their own rhythms that make agreement difficult. Engels' assertion that "in all times of great agitation, the traditional bonds of sexual relations, like all other fetters, are shaken off" (quoted in Weeks, 1985: 252) is scarcely borne out in a period in which the agitation is more *between* groups of minorities than *against* objects of oppression. This agitation is a choice too. And again, it follows a logic that divides and conquers rather than includes.

Queer theory, then, needs to be refocused to take into account the realities of everyday life in a capitalist world system. This means an end to academic posturing, where obfuscation is more valued than strategies for recognition and community-building. In a true sense of the personal as political, this includes a full accounting of the location of position by those generating a new kind of "meta-narrative." The reality of class has to be reintegrated into forms of resistance that include an awareness of difference that is contributory rather than oppositional. Forms of resistance are not styles that can be changed like the color of seasons; there are foundations of economic and energetic inequality that exist and need to be addressed as such.

We hope for a future where arguments around difference and inequality do not exist and are not necessary. The end goal of any movement of resistance to exploitation must be an end to that oppression. The paths of strategy and consciousness are not mere abstractions: they depend on the building of identity around issues that can build real community. In a world where the threat of extinction through war and violence is a very real danger, the need for the identification with social movements that might work toward a society where all are valued, both individually and collectively, is only a beginning, but a necessary one.

# Notes

## Introduction

1 Lyotard's discussion of the "grand" or "meta-narrative" comes from his analysis of postmodernism. While these terms have proved useful for American academics, their genesis comes from a different historical projectory, which will be discussed later in this work.

2 The problem with nomenclature has become even more difficult as attempts are made to include all possible aspects of experience. At a recent Center for Lesbian and Gay Studies conference at the City University of New York, new acronyms became apparent as the Native American definition of "queer" was included (two-spirited), as well as "queer" itself. Thus, some now refer to LGBTTSQ as the correct terminology, making it difficult not only to pronounce but also to justify. I use the term "queer" in this work to refer to the many alternate (and not so alternate) forms of sexual and gendered categories, which will be discussed in more detail in Chapter 2.

3 It is interesting to note that, while gender, sexuality, and class have been constant sources of deconstruction among postmodern and post-structuralist theorists, the category of race has not been challenged. Given what we know about the contingencies of race (the complexities of migration and gene pools), it is safe to assume that this category is viewed as too dangerous to tackle, even for those who claim that the body itself is up for question.

## 1 Crossroads

1 *New York Times*, "Gay Movement Meets Fierce Resistance," Tuesday, July 7, 1998.

2 Here, the example of Carol Vance's (1984) impressive analysis of the Anti-Pornography Commission that was put in place by Ed Meese and the Reagan administration provides an excellent example. In the labeling of pornography and by extension all "deviant" behaviors, the Commission used language and constructs developed by feminist theorists. By incorporating these constructs, the Commission attempted to label all types of sexual behavior, other than idealized heterosexuality, as anti-women, anti-family, and as a danger to society.

3 While academic settings have in general been more accepting of this discussion, the struggle, of course, has not been won. Academic settings are notoriously homophobic, reflected in the reluctance of departments and administrations to include queer studies are part of "diversity" curriculums and in the hiring and tenure of LGBT faculty.

4 This statement, by which she introduced her seminars in culture and personality at Columbia during the 1950s, still has true resonance today. I am grateful to the late Eleanor Leacock, who attended Benedict's seminars, for this personal communication.

5 Note here that Foucault is generally characterized as a post-structuralist, given his questioning of what he calls "structural analysis" (1972: 14). He does note in the *Archaeology of Knowledge*, however, that although "this book, like those that preceded it, does not belong – at least directly, or in the first instance – to the debate on structure (as opposed to genesis, history, development) ... it belongs to that field in which the questions of the human being, consciousness, origin, and the subject emerge, intersect, mingle and separate off. But it would probably not be incorrect to say that the problem of structure arose there too" (1972: 16).

6 Although the dating of modernity differs by interpreter, seventeenth- and eighteenth-century Europe is generally regarded as its height, symbolized by the cries of freedom of the French Revolution, and the quest for knowledge that, it was hoped, would lead to the reform of the "human condition."

7 The quest for reason, too, had its own dangers. Reason for whom and to do what to whom (cf. Wolf, 1999: 35)?

The counter-Enlightenment, by contrast, mistrusted the goals of the French Revolution, particularly those of "liberty," "fraternity," and "equality." Deemed doomed to fail and further fueled by differences over national identity – particularly those of French and German – the proponents of the counter-Enlightenment focused on the necessity of "faith" and "the primordial wisdom of the senses" (Wolf, 1999: 27). While Enlightenment scholars and politicians saw the commonality of humanity as an ultimate point of identity, the counter-Enlightenment leaders argued for differentiation and particularism, especially of identity. Human universalism was rejected. Individual peoples were seen as distinctive "spirits." Thus political and intellectual figures such as Joseph de Maistre, Johann Herder, Wilhelm von Homboldt and later Destrutt de Tracy – the acknowledged creator of a "science" of ideas, or ideology – all dismissed the possibilities of human connection through a common universe. Homboldt, as the Prussian minister of Education, established and implemented the concept of schools that educated elites, thus providing for the creation of separate and superior identities. De Maistre went so far as to state that "The constitution of 1795, just like its predecessors, was made for *man*. But there is no such thing as *man* in the world. I have seen Frenchmen, Italians, Russians ... But as for man, I declare that I have never seen him in my life" (in Wolf, 1999: 28).

8 Wolf's other three modalities are as follows: "One is the power of potency of capability that is seen to adhere in an individual. Power in this Nietzschean sense draws attention to how persons enter into a play of power, but it does not address what that play is about. A second kind of power is manifested in interactions and transactions among people and refers to the ability of an *ego* to impose its will in social action upon an *alter* (the Weberian view). Left unspecified is the nature of the arena in which these interactions go forward. A third modality is that of power that controls the contexts in which people exhibit their capabilities and interact with others. These senses call attention to the instrumentalities through which individuals or groups direct or circumscribe the actions of others within determinate settings. I refer to this as tactical or organizational power ... " (1999: 5–6).

9 The full context of Foucault's remarks are as follows: "The individual is not to be conceived as a sort of elemental nucleus, a primitive atom, a multiple and inert

material on which power comes to fasten or against which it happens to strike, and in doing so subdues or crushes individuals. In fact, it is already one of the prime effects of power that certain bodies, certain gestures, certain discourses, certain desires, come to be identified and constituted as individuals. The individual, that is, is not the site of power; it is, I believe, one of its prime effects. The individual is an effect of power, and at the same time, or precisely to the extent to which it is that effect, it is the element of its articulation ... " (1980: 98).

10  I have noted the connection between the reaction to the movements of 1968, their consequences in France and the development of the postmodern and post-structuralist positions. Mark Lilla (1998) points out that there was a politicizing of philosophy in France during that period with paradoxical effects, for the politicizing of philosophy also meant the devaluation of political philosophy, understood, as he says, "as disciplined and informed reflection about a recognizable domain called politics" (1998: 36). What followed was the questioning of politics itself as it was subjected to the postmodern views that the category, or subject, contained no inherent meaning. The purveyors of this view repositioned politics as they negated all assumed categories, including gender and sexuality, as we have seen. Although they may still consider themselves on the left, and may even still participate in events of resistance, they do not involve themselves in the domain of politics as such.

Derrida, as a founder of this philosophical movement, has declared himself to be on the left but has never elaborated. He has in more recent years tried to regenerate a left-like position, particularly with the publication of *Specters of Marx* (1994), pro-nouncing the "political" to be a category without structural content and positioning Marx as present and absent from politics at the same time. What is needed, he suggests, is a new interpretation of time and being. The radicality of the argument is in convincing us that we need to commit to a way of thinking about an alternative system of existence. Perhaps here we can see the connection that purveys the ten-dency of decontructionist methodology to use the *language* of the left without actually espousing any stated position about the structures of capitalism that produce the all-encompassing domination of power. Social structure becomes so amorphous as to defy engagement, leaving the self to manage alone. The task of structuralism is to find the structures, the binds that formalize the social. But post-structuralists have re-jected even this premise as they emphasize the place of the "difference" and ultimately "choice" in society. For Derrida, any overarching analysis is inherently flawed: there are too many possibilities to generate consistent meaning. Indeed, as Foucault put it in the closing sentence of *Les Mots et les Choses* (published in 1966), "man was a recent invention, that would soon disappear, like a face drawn in the sand" (quoted in Lilla, 1998: 37).

11  This is differentiated from Althusser's earlier critique of the subject (1969). Althusser claimed the subject is simply a product of ideology, individual agency protracted by given historical circumstances. Foucault dismisses the subject altogether. For him, ideology is an element of ideas that has no particular usefulness on its own. Power determines dominant modes of thought, its rationale, and means of repression functioning to provide its own, if temporary, stasis.

12  Baudrillard's critique of the French economic anthropologist Maurice Godelier is notable here, for he seems to be purposefully misinterpreting what Godelier is at-tempting to provide in his analysis of pre-capitalist societies. While Godelier attempts to show, for example, that kinship systems can encompass relations of production, Baudrillard dismisses the claim as more "hide and seek" (1975: 71). He accuses Gode-

lier of attempting to squeeze all formulations into the structures of infra- and super-, while ignoring the context in which the statements were made. It is worth noting that the translator could not find the quotes that Baudrillard attributes to Godelier (see Baudrillard, 1975: 70, note 2). A summary of Godelier's position on economic anthropology can be found in his *Rationality and Irrationality in Economics* (1972).

13  In Baudrillard's words, "The liberation of productive forces is confused with the liberation of man: is this a revolutionary formula or that of political economy itself?" (1975: 23).

14  In focusing on the impossibility of maintaining a "subject," Baudrillard also dismisses any concept of an "other." In his words, "What an absurdity to pretend that men are 'other,' to try to convince them that their deepest desire is to become 'themselves' again! Each man is totally there at each instant. Society also is totally there at each instant. Courderoy, the Luddites, Rimbaud, the Communards, the people of the savage strikes, those of May, 1968 – in every case the revolution does not speak indirectly; they are the revolution, not concepts in transit. Their speech is symbolic and it does not aim at an essence. In these instances, there is speech before history, before politics, before truth, speech before the separation and the future totality. He is truly a revolutionary who speaks of the world as non-separated" (1975: 166).

15  Anderson's (1998) historical rendering of the evolution of Lyotard's position on politics provides an excellent example of the shift from an engagement with radical left political organization to the postmodern position expressing disappointment and disillusionment with the potential power of the proletariat, as put forward in Lyotard's *The Postmodern Condition: A Report on Knowledge* (1984). As Anderson writes, "What the ostensibly scientific framework of Lyotard's 'report on knowledge' let out of view was either the arts or politics. The curiosity of the book lay in the fact that these were his two principal passions as a philosopher. A militant in the far-left group *Socialisme ou Barbarie* for a decade (1954–64) ... Lyotard remained active in its split-off *Pouvoir Ouvrier* for another two years. Breaking with this group when he became convinced the proletariat was no longer a revolutionary subject capable of challenging capitalism, he was active in the university ferment at Nanterre in 1968 and still reinterpreted Marx for contemporary rebels as late as 1969. But with the ebb of insurgency in France, Lyotard's ideas shifted. His first major philosophical work, *Discours, Figure* (1971), advanced a figural rendering of Freudian drives, in opposition to Lacan's linguistic account of the unconscious, as the basis for a theory of art, illustrated by poems and paintings" (Anderson, 1998: 27).

## 2  Making Queer theory

1  The attempt to define "queer," is, for many, antithetical to its purpose. Terry Eagleton (1997) notes that any notion of "closure" tends to make postmodernists nervous, as it suggests, for them, a finality that has become synonymous with dogma (1997: 66–68).

2  Lilla (1998) argues that Derrida and, by extension, his followers were able to maintain their esteemed position in France until the late 1970s, when his star began to fall just as it was rising in the United States. The postcolonial experiments in Africa and Asia had failed, the "communist" regimes collapsed, and the aftermath of 1968 left French radicals seriously divided (Lilla, 1998: 41). On the other hand,

> These same events have had no appreciable effect on American intellectual life, for the simple reason that they pose no challenge to our own self-understanding

> ... That the antihumanism and politics of pure will latent in structuralism and deconstruction ... are philosophically and practically incompatible with liberal principles sounds like an annoying prejudice.

The contrasts between American and European realities are most exacerbated in the protected environment of the academy. Here one is free to develop methodologies of thought that have no discernible consequences, at least as far as one can see. That they actually *are* political in their implicit defense of the logic of capitalism remains unexamined. While parsing words is not inherently inconsistent with a desire for people to accept and include each other, the celebration of difference does not, on its own, provide the necessary basis for seeking alliances. It militates against the actual mobilization that could change the circumstances for all and be applicable in the realm of public life.

3　The literature on Queer theory tends to use the terms "postmodern" and "post-structuralist" together and sometimes interchangeably. I have noted the evolution and distinction of the two theoretical directions in the present work.

4　I assume here that, given the nature of the survey, this statistic also reflects the self-selection of those who vote. Many who are less anxious to admit that they are not "full" members of society choose not to participate in elections, a passive form of resistance that recognizes the place of voting in a system geared towards their continued subjugation.

5　For an exploration of the downward mobility that occurred for the generation of children of this period, see Katherine Newman's "Deindustrialization, Poverty and Downward Mobility: Toward an Anthropology of Economic Disorder" in Shepard Forman (1993), *Diagnosing America*.

6　Susan Raffo's collection *Queerly Classed* (1997) gracefully tries to unite the personal with the political, succeeding at times in highlighting the experience of class and status but often confusing the two categories. More successful is Lancaster and Di Leonardo's *The Gender/Sexuality Reader* (1997), and Donald Morton's *The Material Queer* (1996); these works, which include the political background that initiated the queer movement, are part of a growing reaction to apolitical statements about the place of queers within society.

7　Power is also about consumption. The ability to control others' activities, lifestyle, and labor reflects an ability to *consume* their energy. Symbols of power generated by consumptive acts, then, can promote, in Pierre Bourdieu's words, "Symbolic Violence."

8　For a full discussion of the role and nature of ideology in the construction of action, see Göran Therborn, *The Ideology of Power and the Power of Ideology* (1980).

9　For a comprehensive discussion of the birth of ideology and the "triumph of the bourgeoisie" in France, see Linda Hunt, *Politics, Culture and Class in the French Revolution* (1984).

10　The full statement is:

> In every epoch the ideas of the ruling class are the ruling ideas, that is, the class that is the ruling *material* power of society is at the same time its ruling *intellectual* power. The class having the means of material production has also control over the means of intellectual production, so that it also controls the ideas of those who lack the means of intellectual production. The ruling ideas are nothing more than the ideal expression of the dominant material relationships grasped as ideas, hence of the relationships which make the one class the ruling one and therefore the ideas of its domination. The individuals who comprise the

ruling class possess, among other things, consciousness and thought. Insofar as they rule as a class and determine the extent of an historical epoch, it is self-evident that they do so in its entire range. Among other things they rule also as thinkers and producers of ideas and regulate the production and distribution of the ideas of their age ...

(Marx, 1967: 438)

11 Dalla Costa notes that, "The most recent and monstrous twist to this campaign of extinction [of the person] comes from the extreme example of resistance offered by those who sell parts of their body, a useless container for a labor power that is no longer salable." Where employment and sustainable reproduction become impossible, desperate attempts are made to gain access to the mechanisms of survival: "In Italy, where the sale of organs is banned, press and TV reports in 1993–94 mentioned instances in which people said explicitly that they were willing to break the ban in exchange for obtaining money" (Dalla Costa, 1996: 114).

12 For Burke, there needs to be a consideration of five essential elements – the act, the scene, the agent, the agency, and the purpose – to explore fully these terministic screens. In his words:

> In a rounded statement about motives, you must have some word that names the *act* (names what took place, in thought or deed), and another that names the *scene* (the background of the act, the situation in which it occurred); also, you must indicate what person or kind of person (*agent*) performed the act, what means or instruments he used (*agency*), and the *purpose*.
>
> (quoted in Leacock, 1985: 77)

13 For a full discussion of language as social and political construction, see Kenneth Burke, *Language as Symbolic Action* (1963), David Sapir and J. Christopher Crocker (eds), *The Social Uses of Metaphor: Essays on the Anthropology of Rhetoric* (1944), and Eleanor Leacock, "Individuals and Society in Anthropological Theory" (1985).

14 For an excellent discussion of this phenomenon, see Thomas Frank and Matt Weiland (eds), *Commodify Your Dissent* (1997).

15 As Jeffrey Weeks puts it:

> A slogan such as "bodies are our own" has major implications for the current forms of social regulation of sex. It proposes the justice of sexual self-determination against the law and existing moral positions (including the "re-formed law" of the 1960s and 1970s); but by the very organizational form of its supporters in the women's and gay movements it proclaims the collective nature of the work necessary to realize it. Its major achievement so far has been to bring within the sphere of politics issues that have previously been regarded as scarcely political at all: the questions of identity, pleasure, consent and choice.
>
> (Weeks, 1995: 32)

16 Berman quoted in Willis (1993). Willis, in critiquing the pessimism of postmodernism, argues that

> The market is the source of a permanent and contradictory revolution in everyday culture which sweeps away old limits and dependencies. The markets' restless search to find and make new appetites raises, wholesale, the popular

currency of symbolic aspiration. The currency may be debased or inflationary, but aspirations now circulate, just as do commodities. That circulation irrevocably makes or finds its own worlds.

The style and media theorists – and terrorists – of the left and right see only market incandescence. They warn us of an immanent semiotic implosion of all that is real. They call us to a strange rejection of all that glitters and shimmers over the dark landscape, as if it *were* the landscape. But this usually metropolitan neurosis is nothing more than a bad case of idealist theorists' becoming the victims of their own nightmares.

(1993: 27)

### 3  Considering sex, gender, and difference

1 For those interested in the importance of the global economy, particularly significant was Nash's "Ethnographic Aspects of the World Capitalist System" (1981) and Nash and Fernandez-Kelley's *Women, Men and the International Division of Labor* (1983), both of which reflect on situated communities in the light of an expanding world system.

2 In particular, the posing of dichotomies has taken place in direct reaction to the rejection of a dialectical methodology which is more directly tied to a rejection of Marx and Engels within the academy than to a consideration and critique of the methodology itself. Many have integrated dialectics, and even Trotsky's conception of uneven and combined development, without acknowledging the source or its implications (see, for example, Marshall Sahlins and Elman Service's *Evolution and Culture* (1970)).

3 This aspect of gender is treated in more detail in Chapter 4.

4 There is a broad literature that has attempted to redefine the terms of research and explanation. See, for example, Cole and Scribner's "Introduction" to L.S. Vygotsky's *Mind in Society* (1978); Leacock's "Interpreting the Origins of Gender Inequality: Conceptual and Historical Problems" (1983), and her "Introduction" to Engels, *Origin of the Family, Private Property and the State* (1972); Ross and Rapp's "Sex and Society: A Research Note from Social History and Anthropology" (1997); and Epstein's "Gay Politics, Ethnic Identity: The Limits of Social Constructionism" (1987).

5 For example, Eagleton remarks that "The oppression of women is a matter of gender, but women are oppressed *as women*, which involves the kind of body one happens to have. Being bourgeois or proletarian, by contrast, is not a biological affair or law" (1997: 94)

6 Note that Butler (1991: 32) critiques the "speculation" of Engels, and locates all "socialist feminism" as rooted in the work of Lévi-Strauss' structural anthropology. Like Wittig, she notes that subjectivity and difference have not been central aspects of Marxist theory, while failing to acknowledge that these foci have not been the central aspects of theory *in general*. The need to attack Marxist theory is significant for politics. What is most notable for the present discussion, however, is the dismissal of important work that has been accomplished in providing data for Engels' work that can be found in the critiques of structuralism taken up by many feminist and Marxist anthropologists. Butler does not acknowledge that the universal subjugation of women is not a given in anthropology, but has been the subject of intense debate for the past twenty years. For an overview, see the many articles that have appeared in *Dialectical Anthropology*, and in the collected articles of Eleanor Leacock in *Myths of Male Dominance* (1981). The implications and evolution of these anti-Marxist points of view is taken up in more detail in Chapter 3.

7 To be clear, Seidman states that the title is coincidental, "and is not intended as a response to Butler's seminal text" (1997: ix). He also makes apparent, however, that Butler's work has made possible his own, to the extent that his aim is to "expose the way social theory, in particular sociological and lesbian/gay theory, has resisted conceptualizing difference as a central axis of subjectivity and social life."

8 This article appears as Chapter 2 of *Difference Troubles* (Seidman, 1997).

9 Seidman cites sociological writers (1997: 110) and then implicitly rejects them, noting instead the antagonism towards Marxism in the new social movements that were more concerned with individual voices and cultural critiques.

10 Lancaster and Di Leonardo, going against the grain of Queer theorists, go on to point out that,

> In the course of the 1980s, a substantial current of gender and sexuality studies withdrew to a narrow, disengaged, and frequently idealistic conception of social constructionism. Postmodernism habitually and synecdochically misidentified Marxism and political economy with older, reductionist, mechanistic schools of thought ... and thus often simply ignored political–economic contexts in their writing. Ironically, it was in the same decade that work in political economy became increasingly historically sophisticated ... and took on culture, language, race and gender as key analytic categories.
>
> (1997: 4)

11 This refusal to declare her hostility to political economy is, of course, also a declaration. While criticizing others for "essentializing" their point of view, she naturalizes her own.

12 As Wolf (1999) explains,

> class and classness are better understood in terms of relations that develop historically within a social field. That field subsumes diverse kinds of people, rearranges them, and causes them to respond to new ways of marshaling social labor. One can then speak of the "making" of a class (as did E.P. Thompson in *The Making of the English Working Class* [1980]) out of disparate groups of people, who bear diverse cultural heritages and yet must adjust them to the requirements of a new social order. Similarly, a class may be "unmade" and its members scattered and reallocated to different groupings and strata.
>
> (1999: 65)

13 As Eagleton remarks,

> To register the patronizing quality of this [kind of] cultural determinism, one has only to ask oneself whether it would be so readily asserted of, say, African Americans or the Liverpool Irish that they were the mere prisoners of their unthinking conventions, tribalist in the most pejorative sense of the term. Yet something like this is sometimes claimed of, say, American academia, where one can get away with calling them a code-bound tribe because it seems an iconoclastic deflation of Western rationalist pretensions, and so anti-ethnocentric rather than objectionable.
>
> (1997: 89)

14 If we follow Scott's own logic, then, we can only assume that she, too, refuses to be identified (or believes she has no identification). The caveat that one *should* state where they are proceeding from in their analysis does not make analysis impossible. Where does her usefulness lie then as a historian? Is it possible that this is something that she herself has questioned?

15 Here I do not mean "the reality" pejoratively, in a sense of "get real," but rather in the sense of a "realization" that we are all part of the culture, the social. This fact is inescapable, and to concentrate on "difference" negates "the real" as a fact.

16 For an interesting exploration of these questions of subjectivism, language, philosophy, and anthropology, see E. Gellner, *Language and Solitude: Wittgenstein, Malinowski and the Habsburg Dilemma* (1998).

## 4  Capitalism and its transgressors

1 Many historical and anthropological analyses have documented this process of alienation and attempts by managers of capital to enforce these divisions. Bertell Ollman (1971) provides a discussion of the concept of alienation in his *Alienation, Marx's Conception of Man in Capitalist Society*.

   For a comprehensive analysis of the ethnographic data, see June Nash, "Ethnographic Aspects of the World Capitalist System" (1981). For an analysis of the colonial period, see Talal Asad (ed.), *Anthropology and the Colonial Encounter* (1973). For more recent analyses, see June Nash, *We Eat the Mines and the Mines Eat Us* (1979), and June Nash and Fernández-Kelly, *Women, Men and the International Division of Labor* (1983). An excellent example from the United States context is provided by Herbert Gutman in his *Work, Culture and Society* (1977).

2 This is not to deny the obvious consequence that with the emergence of the categories of gay and lesbian comes a new kind of oppression that is discussed throughout this work. It is only an exposition of the development of categories that we now too often assume are historically and culturally universal.

3 This idea of the oversexed "other," derived from the Protestant ethic, persists into the present day. Note the generalizations around gay male sexuality, promiscuity, and deviant sexual behavior. As a cultural phenomenon, the existence of alternatives to idealized heterosexuality has often been used to explain the "otherness" of populations, whether they are racial "others," gender non-conformists, or simply those who fail to conform to the idealized norm.

4 Pearce and Roberts note that homosexuality in general was seen as weakening the internal character of the country, an ideology that became grounded in a series of military scandals that coincided with the increasing loss of British colonies. This was the context for the prosecution of Oscar Wilde for indecent acts, and a renewed prosecution likewise of army soldiers. Britain had lost the first Boer War, and after a poor showing in the second Boer War, the government, backed up by the media, declared that the health and obedience of soldiers was a major problem. The moral superiority of Christianity was thereby reasserted.

5 This brings to mind the now-popular notion of so-called "virtual communities." Driven by bits of information without providing the means for a holistic understanding, they have no material means to sustain them. They may be successful in operating as a community in the short term (the growth of on-line consuming and dating services, for example), or even as tools for resistance (the derailing of the Multilateral Agreement on Investment). But these are *instances* of community in the loosest sense

– they cannot be reinforced without history or physical space. They lose their members as soon as the issue under discussion fades. In short, they cannot reproduce themselves, or act in unison beyond the purveying of information, quickly outdated and rendered obsolete.

6 This is discussed in more detail in Chapter 5. The preoccupation of post-structuralists with disengagement as an act of resistance, of parody as re-description, works against the formation of community just as much as it (falsely) pretends to work *toward* self-actualization. That we are members of a society *should* be self-evident. How power and domination are actualized and maintained through capitalist control is both an empirical and a political question.

7 Michael Signorile's work is a particularly strong example of the cultural evolution of aesthetic standards in gay culture: all men are created equal – from desperate young men for hire to Hollywood power brokers. But what really matters is what you are wearing. Even the cover of *Life on the Outside* (1997) reveals a very particular situated position steeped in images of consumer correctness. He thus further positions himself as the prototype of a continuing A-list presence, with a "steady" boyfriend, a dog, and, one assumes, a white picket fence. There is no affiliation here with discrimination, with the role of the community, or any analysis of the "ghetto" and its purposes.

8 Cross-market approaches to advertising are becoming more pervasive. The Calvin Klein underwear ads, appealing to both heterosexual and queer audiences, are produced by the same advertising agency.

9 I refer the reader to Lutz and Collins' (1993) work on race and gender in *National Geographic Magazine*.

10 For an interesting account of this phenomenon, see Arjun Appadurai's *The Social Life of Things* (1986).

11 In like form, Baudrillard stresses that

> we don't realize how much the current indoctrination into systemic and organized consumption is the *equivalent and the extension, in the Twentieth Century, of the great indoctrination of rural populations into industrial labor, which occurred throughout the nineteenth century*. The same process of rationalization of productive forces, which took place in the nineteenth century in the sector of *production*, is accomplished, in the twentieth century, in the sector of *consumption*. Having socialized the masses of labor into a labor force, the industrial system had to go further in order to fulfill itself and to socialize masses (that is, to control them) into a force of consumption.
>
> (1975: 54)

12 "Middletown" is not the real name of the community. The ethnographic study was meant to represent a *community as sample*, that is, a representation of mainstream American life.

13 Diane Clark, in her "Commodity Lesbianism" (1995) makes the point that lesbians have not until recently been targeted as a consuming group for niche marketing because they have not been easily identifiable as a social group or seen as powerful in the economic arena. She also notes that, while several waves of the feminist movement have shunned fashion as an indicator of identity, it has recently become a site of resistance and self-representation. The growth of women's economic power, particularly in urban areas, has led to a more concentrated effort by advertisers to address lesbians and the fashion trends that are seeping into the heterosexual mainstream,

such as the recent appearance of butch-femme styles as part of a campy renaissance. For advertisers and capitalist managers alike, lesbian, and even transgender, fashion is fine; politics is not.

14  The most classic analyses of this integration of foreign traits into local cultures have been done on Latin American cultures, particularly the Aztecs. For an interesting recent interpretation of the same phenomenon in the context of globalization, see Xudong Zhang, "Postmodernism and Post-Socialist Society: Cultural Politics in China After the 'New Era' " (1999).

15  Altman's "On Global Queering" (1996) drew a variety of interesting responses, mostly objecting to the assumption of homogenization and the global imposition of "queer" as defined by Americans. The argument that there is a diffusion of cultural traits tends to obscure issues of class and the acquisition of status. While Altman's interesting observations cannot be faulted for noting a phenomenon of cultural accommodation that is indeed occurring, the questions of for whom it is occurring and why remain to be explored.

## 5  Meta-identity, performativity, and internalized homophobia

1  And, by implication, her own position.

2  Butler, unlike some of her peers, does not question the use of the "I" as central. See her "Contingent Foundations" in Seyla Benhabib *et al.*'s *Feminist Contentions* (1995).

3  This view is familiar. The arguments concerning "modes of production" constituted debates about whether the *mode* of production changed when relations of production differed. As Eleanor Leacock succinctly put it: "Changing your underwear does not constitute a change in the mode of production, although it may constitute a change in your relationships" (personal communication).

4  It is notable that Butler accepts Lévi-Strauss' analysis of women as "gifts" in systems of exchange, therefore bypassing the methodological problems and the ethnographic data that feminist anthropologists have debated (see, for example, Leacock, 1981; Leacock and Nash, 1981; Silverblatt, 1987; Siskind, 1978). Eleanor Leacock, as one of the founders of a feminist anthropology, wrote that Lévi-Strauss assumed a universal female subjugation and a primarily masculine society. But instead of simply inserting a theoretical premise, she provided data on cultures where these assumptions were not played out, arguing that "Adaptive functions, or end results ... do not account for origins" (1981: 230). Assuming a "masculine society," Leacock argued that Lévi-Strauss did not consider women's social or sexual drives:

> That women ... should be things that were exchanged ... was the only means of overcoming the contradiction by which the same woman was seen under two incompatible aspects: on the one hand, as the object of personal desire, thus exciting sexual and proprietorial instincts, and, on the other, as the object of the desire of others, and seen as such, i.e., as a means of binding others through alliance with them.
>
> (Leacock, 1981: 233)

Although Lévi-Strauss' own logic is based on a construction that assumes matrilocal societies to be rare, his belief relies upon a mislabeling of societies. As Leacock further notes, "Matrilineal–matrilocal societies constitute forty-one percent of the eighty-four matrilineal societies that appear in George Peter Murdock's 'world ethnographic sample' " (1981: 235). The very terminology that Lévi-Strauss invokes symbolizes an *ideology* derived from his own theoretical position rather than from data that exist in the ethnographic world – assumptions that Butler accepts because they fit into her own schemata, the subtext of which positions women in an ahistorical omnipotent world of power embodied by men.

## 6  From culture to action

1  Valocchi (n.d.) makes the interesting point that, in reality, there is a blurring of "old" and "new" social movements, for "class based organizations tried to organize people around 'new social movement' areas of peace, civil rights, and youth justice, and some of the folks in the new social movement areas of peace, civil rights, and youth mobilization saw these issues in class terms" (n.d.: 7).

2  It is useful here to re-employ Bourdieu's notion of practices and habitus as a vehicle to see, theoretically, how divergent experiences can be objectively analyzed. For Bourdieu, habitus involves

> the life-style characteristic of an agent or class of agents, that is, the unity hidden under the diversity and multiplicity of the set of practices performed in fields governed by different logics and therefore inducing different forms of realization, in accordance with the formula: [(habitus) (capital)] + field = practice ... So it is necessary to reconstruct what has been taken apart, first by way of verification but also in order to rediscover the kernel of truth in the approach characteristic of common-sense knowledge, namely, the intuition of the systematic nature of life-styles and the whole set which they constitute. To do this, one must return to the practice-unifying and practice-generating principle, i.e., class-habitus, the internalized form of class conditions and of the conditionings it entails ...
>
> (Bourdieu, 1982: 101)

3  These are, of course, crude generalities, but they nonetheless express common conceptions about divisions within the queer movement.

4  That is not to say that there were not other conceptions of minority rights that were put forward. One of the first decisions by the leaders of the Russian Revolution was to ban discrimination based on sex, and Lenin and Trotsky both committed time and writing to the analysis of discrimination, behavior, and consciousness in a revolutionary setting. See, for example, Trotsky's *Problems of Everyday Life* (1973). In his essay "Not by Politics Alone," he reminds us that

> When Lenin says that at the present moment our work is less concerned with politics than with culture, we must be quite clear about the terms he uses ... Even the advice of Lenin to shift our interests from politics to culture is a piece of political advice ... It is quite obvious here that the word "politics" is used here in two different meanings: firstly, in a wide materialist and dialectical sense, as the totality of all guiding principles, methods, systems that determine collective activities in all domains of public life; and, on the other hand, in a restricted sense, specifying a definite part of public activity, directly concerned with the struggle for power and opposed to economic work, to the struggle for culture, etc.
>
> (1973: 18)

5  I am indebted here to the observations of Eric Wolf, who uses Gregory Bateson's classic analysis of Nuer social organization to show how the transfer of energy among social institutions strengthens some to the detriment of others. Lineages may gain at the expense of family or household organization, for example, and this transfer always implies tension. He proposes that Marx and Freud both recognized this form of energy transfer and source of conflict in different systems, stating that for both,

> the *form* of the arguments are quite similar, although applied to different levels or systems of phenomena. Marx argued that the imposition of class distinctions gave rise to a contradiction between exploiters and exploited, with grave and ultimately fateful consequences for the system of social relations. Freud argued that the imposition of the superego – represented by parental authority figures within the developing organism – gave rise to barely manageable discontents, likely at any time to break through in self-destructive or destructive paroxysms. The model underlying their reasoning is that of a closed hydraulic system, in which energy held back at one point will inevitably exert pressure in some other salient. We do not have to adopt the notion of closed systems – societal or individual – to make use of their underlying understanding that domination and repression give rise to forces that become socially and individually active, both in the public and the personal realm.
>
> ("Ideas and Power," MS, 1985: 13–14)

(See also Wolf's *Envisioning Power: Ideologies of Dominance and Crisis* (1999).)

6  For a more detailed explanation of the use of energy as social process, see Leslie White, *The Science of Culture* (1949).

7  For a comprehensive and clear discussion of the role of trade and the division of labor in the evolution of mental work, see Eleanor Leacock's "Introduction" to Engels' *Origin of the Family, Private Property and the State* (1972).

8  In his words, "the realism of those who insist that it is people, not cultures who vote, speak English, enamel their nails, loathe milk, etc., is a pathetic form of pseudo-realism that has no place in science" (1949: 408).

9  Brennan notes that both Heidegger and Benjamin referred to the use of technology in the development of society. Benjamin, in particular, focused on aspects of power, and related energy directly to the foundations of capitalism and imperialism, and the political implications of redirecting energy into proletarian arenas.

10  The movements continued to develop throughout the nineteenth century, through the decades of the twentieth century and into the present day. They continue to generate community, and communities reinforce their development. The French Revolution, the Russian Revolution, various movements for national independence, and the social struggles of the 1960s and 1970s all provide models for organization.

11  For excellent and detailed histories of gay and lesbian movements, see Adam (1995), Katz (1976), and D'Emilio (1983). Much of this discussion is informed by their work, and the history presented here is indebted to Adams' work.

12  For a detailed history of the Daughters of Bilitis, as well as probably the best history of lesbian movements available, see Faderman (1995).

13  For a discussion of the effects of the rise of the service sector and the flight of industry from US communities, see my *In the Wake of the Giant* (1998).

14  Esther Newton (1993) points out that western Europe has a longer history of movements with generally socialist goals. This difference from movements in the

United States results from a longer history of union activism, movements for social democracy, and direct resistance to the development and implementation of capitalism.

15 Claim made at the Human Rights Campaign dinner in Cleveland, Ohio, March, 1999.

16 In a timely example that resonates with the argument against the mainstreaming of queer politics, the August 26, 1999 edition of *The New York Times* reports the case of "An Unlikely 'Don't Tell' Target: Lawmaker May Face Discharge." A conservative Republican member of the Arizona State Legislature (and the Gay Republican Log Cabin), who is also a member of the Army Reserve, is being threatened with dismissal from military service because he argued against a bill that would have barred the use of public funds to pay for health benefits for same-sex partners. Contending that his public admission of his gay identity provides means for dismissal under Clinton's "Don't Ask, Don't Tell" policy, he is currently being investigated. As *The New York Times* reports,

> Under that policy, recruiters are barred from asking applicants about sexual orientation, and commanders are forbidden to undertake investigations of suspected homosexuals unless there is significant evidence of at least an intent to engage in homosexual acts.
>
> On the other hand, homosexuals are forbidden to disclose their orientation in a pubic setting; indeed, their doing so is considered evidence of homosexual conduct.
>
> (*New York Times*, Thursday, August 26, 1999: 1ff.)

17 As Martin Duberman succinctly sums up

> you cannot adopt (or pretend to adopt) the dominant values of a culture and at the same time hope to reorder those values. The token adjustments that power brokers grant from time to time are insufficient to dilute (and – whether by design or otherwise – in the long term strengthen) our society's instinctive distaste for substantial change, its zeal for homogenization and its entrenched suspicion of the very diversity it rhetorically defends.
>
> (1996: 46)

## Conclusion: theory, politics, and the community

1 For a fuller discussion of the concept of part-cultures, see Eric R. Wolf, "Specific Aspects of Plantation Systems in the New World: Community Subcultures and Social Class," in *Plantation Systems of the New World* (1959). Here Wolf uses the concept of part-cultures as developed by Alfred Kroeber, who recognized the connection between peasant societies and the larger social system.

2 Civil society here is used in the broadest sense, as an alternative, for example, to Habermas' notion of the "bourgeois public sphere" and its degeneration (Habermas, 1991). It is not an attempt to relocate public action in the political realm of the "High European Enlightenment," but in the actions of organizations and communities outside of direct state control. While these organizations and communities are, of course, affected by the dominant ideologies that persist, they act on those ideologies in their own terms, generating the forms of practice that can act against the power of the state and the multinational organization of capital.

3 As Gordon (1996) points out, 1990s real wages in the United States are below those of 1975. For a full discussion of how profit has been distributed and its effects on the standard of living, see his *Fat and Mean* (1996).

4 June Nash, *Mayas in the New World Disorder* (forthcoming).

5 As Simon Watney argues, Queer theory has even marginalized the phenomenon of AIDS for the sake of high theory (quoted in Seidman, 1997: 141).

# Bibliography

Abelove, Henry, Barale, M.A. and Halperin, D.M. (1993), *The Lesbian and Gay Studies Reader*, New York: Routledge.

Adam, Barry (1978), *The Survival of Domination: Inferiorization and Everyday Life*, New York: Elsevier.

——(1985), "Structural Foundations of the Gay World," *Comparative Studies in Society and History*, 27, pp. 658–671.

——(1995), *The Rise of a Gay and Lesbian Movement*, New York: Twayne Publishers.

Aglietta, Michael (1979), *A Theory of Capitalist Regulation: The U.S. Experience*, London: New Left Books.

Almaguer, Tomás (1993), "Chicano Men: A Cartography of Homosexual Identity and Behavior," in H. Abelove, M.A. Barale and D. Halperin, eds., *The Lesbian and Gay Studies Reader*, New York: Routledge.

Althusser, L. (1969), *For Marx*, London: New Left Books.

Altman, Dennis (1983), *The Homosexualization of America, the Americanization of the Homosexual*, New York: St Martins.

——(1996), "On Global Queering," *Australian Humanities Review*, July.

Anderson, Perry (1976), *Considerations on Western Marxism*, London: New Left Books.

——(1998), *The Origins of Postmodernity*, London: Verso.

Angelides, Stephen (1994), "The Queer Intervention," *Melbourne Journal of Politics*, 22.

Appadurai, Arjun, ed. (1986), *The Social Life of Things*, Cambridge: Cambridge University Press.

Appiah, Anthony and Gates, Henry Louis eds. (1995), *Identities*, Chicago: University of Chicago Press.

Arensberg, Conrad (n.d.), "Common Sense," U.S. State Department, Foreign Services Office.

Arrighi, Giovanni (1994), *The Long Twentieth Century*, London: Verso.

Barthes, Roland (1990), *The Fashion System*, Berkeley: University of California Press.

Baudrillard, Jean (1975), *The Mirror of Production*, St Louis: Telos Press.

——(1981), *For a Critique of the Political Economy of the Sign*, St Louis: Telos Press.

——(1983), *In the Shadow of the Silent Majorities*, New York: Autonomedia.

——(1984), *Simulations*, New York: Autonomedia.

Beemyn, Brett and Eliason, Mickey (1996), *Queer Studies: A Lesbian, Gay, Bisexual, and Transgender Anthology*, New York: New York University Press.

Bell, Vikki (1999), "On Speech, Race and Melancholia: An Interview with Judith Butler," *Theory, Culture and Society*, 16(2), 163–174.

Beneria, Lourdes and Roldán, Martha (1987), *The Crossroads of Class and Gender: Industrial Homework, Subcontracting and Household Dynamics in Mexico City*, Chicago: University of Chicago Press.

Benhabib, Seyla (1992), *Situating the Self: Gender, Community, and Post-Modernism in Contemporary Ethics*, New York: Routledge.

Benhabib, Seyla, Butler, Judith, Cornell, Drucilla and Fraser, Nancy (1995), *Feminist Contentions*, New York: Routledge.

Berlant, Lauren (1997), *The Queen of America Goes to Washington City: Essays on Sex and Citizenship*, Durham: Duke University Press.

Berman, Marshall (1982), *All that is Solid Melts into Air: The Experience of Modernity*, New York: Simon and Schuster.

Betsky, Aaron (1997), *Queer Space: Architecture and Same-Sex Desire*, New York: William Morrow and Co.

Blacking, John, ed. (1977), *The Anthropology of the Body*, A.S.A. Monographs 15, London: Academic Press.

Blackwood, Evelyn, ed. (1989), *The Many Faces of Homosexuality: Anthropological Approaches to Homosexual Behavior*, New York: Harrington Park Press.

Bloch, Maurice (1997), *The Way They Think: Anthropological Approaches to Cognition, Memory, and Literacy*, Boulder, CO: Westview Press.

Bourdieu, Pierre (1977), *Outline of a Theory of Practice*, Cambridge: Cambridge University Press.

——(1982), *Distinction*, Cambridge, MA: Harvard University Press.

——(1998), "A Reasoned Utopia and Economic Fatalism," *New Left Review*, 228, pp. 225–230.

Bourdieu, Pierre, and Wacquant, Loîc J.D. (1992), *An Invitation to Reflexive Sociology*, Chicago: University of Chicago Press.

Brecher, Jeremy, Costello, T. and Smith, Brendan (2000), "The Road from Seattle," *Z Magazine*, January, pp. 40–43.

Brennan, Teresa (1993), *History After Lacan*, London: Routledge.

Burke, Kenneth (1963), *Language as Symbolic Action*, Berkeley: University of California Press.

Butler, Judith (1990), *Gender Trouble: Feminism and the Subversion of Identity*, New York: Routledge.

——(1991), "Imitation and Gender Insubordination," in *Inside/Out: Lesbian Theories, Gay Theories*, ed. Diana Fuss, New York: Routledge.

——(1992), "Contingent Foundations: Feminism and the Question of 'Postmodernism' " in *Feminists Theorize the Political*, ed. J. Butler and J.W. Scott, New York: Routledge, pp. 3–21.

——(1993a), "Imitation and Gender Insubordination," in H. Abelove, M.A. Barale and D. Halperin, eds., *The Lesbian and Gay Studies Reader*, New York: Routledge, pp. 307–320

——(1993b), *Bodies that Matter*, New York: Routledge.

——(1994), "Against Proper Objects," *Differences: A Journal of Feminist Cultures Studies*, 1(1), pp. 17–32.

——(1995), "Contingent Foundations," in Seyla Benhabib, Judith Butler, Drucilla Cornell and Nancy Fraser, *Feminist Contentions*, New York: Routledge.

——(1997), *Executed Speech: A Politics of the Performative*, New York: Routledge.

——(1998), "Merely Cultural?" *New Left Review*, 227, pp. 33–44.

——(1999), "A 'Bad Writer' Bites Back," *New York Times* (Op. Ed.), March 20, 1999.

Carchedi, Guglielmo (1975), "On the Economic Identification of the New Middle Class," *Economy and Society*, 4(1), pp. 1–86.

Carrithers, M., Collins, S. and Lukes, S. (1994), *The Category of the Person*, Cambridge: Cambridge University Press.

Castells, Manuel (1983), *The City and the Grassroots*, Berkeley: University of California Press.

——(1997), *The Power of Identity*, Malden, MA: Blackwell.

Chandler, Alfred (1990), *Scale and Scope: The Dynamics of Industrial Capitalism*, Cambridge, MA: Harvard University Press.

Clare, Elizabeth (1998), "Losing Home," In Susan Raffo, ed., *Queerly Classed*, Boston: South End Press.

Clark, Diane (1995), "Commodity Lesbianism," in H. Abelove, M.A. Barale, and D. Halperin, eds., *The Lesbian and Gay Studies Reader*, New York: Routledge.

Cockburn, Alexander (1995), "'Win Win' with Bruce Babbit: the Clinton Administration Meets the Environment," *New Left Review*, 201.

Cohen, Jean (1985), "Strategy or Identity: New Theoretical Paradigms and Contemporary Social Movements," *Social Research*, 52, pp. 663–716.

Cole, Michael and Scribner, Sylvia (1978), "Introduction" to L.S. Vygotsky, *Mind in Society*, Cambridge, MA: Harvard University Press.

Corbridge, S., Thrift, N., and Martin, R., eds. (1994), *Money, Power and Space*, Oxford: Blackwell.

Creekmur, Corey and Doty, Alexander, eds. (1995), *Out in Culture: Gay, Lesbian and Queer Essays on Popular Culture*, Durham: Duke University Press.

Crighton, Elizabeth and Mason, David (1986), "Solidarity and the Green: the Rise of New Social Movements in East and West Europe," in *Research in Social Movements, Conflict and Change*, ed. Lois Kreisberg, Greenwich: JAI Press.

Curthoys, Jean (1997), *Feminist Amensias*, New York: Routledge.

Dalla Costa, María Rosa (1996), "Capitalism and Reproduction," *Capitalism, Native, Society*, 7(4), December.

Davis, Shelton (1977), *Victims of the Miracle: Development and the Indians of Brazil*, New York: Cambridge University Press.

Deere, Carmen Diana (1977), "Changing Social Relations of Production and Peruvian Women's Work," *Latin American Perspectives*, 4, pp. 48–69.

D'Emilio, John (1983), *Sexual Politics, Sexual Communities*, Chicago: University of Chicago Press.

——(1997), "Capitalism and Gay Identity," in R.N. Lancaster and M. Di Leonardo, eds., *The Gender/Sexuality Reader*, New York: Routledge.

D'Emilio, J. and Freedman, E. (1988), *Intimate Matters*, New York: Harper and Row.

Derrida, Jacques (1976), *Of Grammatology*, trans. Gayatri Chakravorty Spivak, Baltimore: Johns Hopkins University Press.

——(1994), *Specters of Marx*, New York: Routledge.

Dews, Peter (1984), "Power and Subjectivity in Foucault," *New Left Review*, 144, March/April.

Di Leonardo, Micaela (1991), *Gender at the Crossroads of Knowledge: Feminist Anthropology in the Postmodern Era*, Berkeley: University of California Press.

——(1993), "What a Difference Political Economy Makes," *Anthropological Quaterly*, 66(2), pp. 76–80.

Doty, Alexander (1993), *Making Things Perfectly Queer: Interpreting Mass Culture*, Minneapolis: University of Minnesota Press.

Duberman, Martin (1993), *Stonewall*, New York: Dutton.

——(1996), *Midlife Queer: Autobiography of a Decade, 1971–1981*, Madison: University of Wisconsin Press.

——(1997), *Queer Representations: Reading Lives, Reading Cultures: A Center for Lesbian and Gay Studies Book*, New York: New York University Press.

Duggan, Lisa (1992), "Making it Perfectly Queer," *Socialist Review*, 22(1).

Duyal, Len (1993), "Thinking About Human Need," *New Left Review*, 202.

Dynes, W.R. and Donaldson, S. (1992), *Ethnographic Studies of Homosexuality*, New York: Garland.

Eagleton, Terry (1986), *Against the Grain: Essays 1975–1985*, London: Verso.

——(1990), *The Ideology of the Aesthetic*, Oxford: Blackwell.

——(1991), *Ideology*, London: Verso.

——(1997), *The Illusions of Postmodernism*, Oxford: Blackwell.

*Economist* (1990), January 1.

Edelman, Lee (1994), *Homographesis: Essays in Gay Literary and Cultural Theory*, New York: Routledge.

Eder, Klaus (1985), "The New Social Movements: Moral Crusades, Political Pressure Groups or Social Movements?" *Social Research*, 52(4), pp. 28–42.

——(1993), *The New Politics of Class: Social Movements and Cultural Dynamics in Advanced Societies*, London: Routledge.

Edgar, Andrew and Sedgwick, Peter, eds. (1999), *Key Concepts in Cultural Theory*, London: Routledge.

Edstron, A. and Gailbraith, J. (1993), "Transfer of Managers as a Coordination and Control in Multinational Organizations," in G. Hedlund, ed., *Organisation of Transnational Corporations*, London: Routledge, pp. 222–243.

Emilio, John (1992), *Making Trouble*, London: Routledge.

Emilio, John and Freedman, Estelle (1988), *Intimate Matters*, New York: Harper and Row.

Engels, Friedrich (1935), *Ludwig Feuerbach and the Nature of Classical German Philosophy*, New York: International Publishers.

Epstein, Steven (1987), "Gay Politics, Ethnic Identity: The Limits of Social Constructionism," *Socialist Review*, 17, pp. 9–54.

Escoffier, Jeffrey (1985), "Sexual Revolution and the Politics of Gay Identity," *Socialist Review*, 15, pp. 119–153.

——(1990), "Inside the Ivory Closet: The Challenges Facing Lesbian and Gay Studies," *Outlook: National Lesbian and Gay Quarterly*, 10, pp. 40–48.

——(1998), *American Homo*, Berkeley: University of California Press.

Etienne, Mona and Leacock, E. (1980), *Women and Colonization: Anthropological Perspectives*, New York: Praeger.

Ewen, Stuart (1976), *Captains of Consciousness: Advertising and the Social Roots of the Consumer Culture*, New York: McGraw-Hill.

——(1988), *All Consuming Images: The Politics of Style in Contemporary Culture*, New York: Basic Books.

Faderman, Lillian (1995), *Surpassing the Love of Men: Romantic Friendship and Love Between Women from the Renaissance to the Present*, London: The Women's Press.

Fanon, Frantz (1952), *Black Skin, White Masks*, London: Pluto Press.

Feinberg, Leslie (1996), *Transgender Warriors*, Boston: Beacon Press.

Forman, Shepard, ed. (1993), *Diagnosing America*, Ann Arbor: University of Michigan Press.

Foucault, Michel (1972), *The Archaeology of Knowledge and the Discourse on Language*, New York: Pantheon Books.

——(1980), *Power/Knowledge: Selected Interviews and Other Writings*, ed. Colin Gordon, New York: Pantheon Press.

——(1982), "The Subject and Power," in Herbert Dreyfus and Paul Rabinow, *Beyond Structuralism and Hermeneutics*, Chicago: University of Chicago Press.

——(1990), *The History of Sexuality*, 3 vols, New York: Vintage.

——(1995), *Discipline and Punish*, New York: Vintage.

Frank, Thomas and Weiland, Matt, eds. (1997), *Commodify Your Dissent*, New York: W.W. Norton and Co.

Fraser, Nancy (1998), "Heterosexism, Misrecognition and Capitalism: A Response to Judith Butler," *New Left Review*, 228, pp. 140–150.

Fraser, Nancy and Nicholson, Linda (1989), "Social Criticism without Philosophy: An Encounter Between Feminism and Postmodernism," *Social Text*, 7(3), pp. 83–104.

Fuss, Diana (1991), *Inside/Out*, New York: Routledge.

Galler, Roberts (1984), "The Myth of the Perfect Body," in C.F. Vance, ed., *Pleasure and Danger*, New York: Routledge.

Gamson, Joshua (1994), *Claims to Fame: Celebrity in Contemporary America*, Berkeley: University of California Press.

Geertz, Clifford (1973), *The Interpretation of Cultures*, New York: Basic Books.

——(1983), *Local Knowledge*, New York: Basic Books.

Gellner, Ernest (1987), *Culture, Identity and Politics*, Cambridge: Cambridge University Press.

——(1998), *Language and Solitude: Wittgenstein, Malinowski and the Hapsburg Dilemma*, Cambridge: Cambridge University Press.

George, S. and Sabelli, F. (1994), *Faith and Credit*, London: Penguin.

Gereffi, Gary (1994), "Capitalism, Development, and Global Commodity Chains," in L. Sklair, ed., *Capitalism and Development*, London: Routledge, pp. 211–231.

Gitlin, Todd (1995), *The Twilight of Common Dreams*, New York: Henry Holt.

Gluckman, Amy *et al.* (1997), *Homo Economics: Capitalism, Community, and Lesbian and Gay Life*, New York: Routledge.

Godelier, Maurice (1972), *Rationality and Irrationality in Economics*, New York: Monthly Review Press.

Goodenough, W.H. (1970), *Description of Comparison in Cultural Anthropology*, Chicago: Aldine.

Gordon, David (1996), *Fat and Mean*, New York: The Free Press, Martin Kessler Books.

Gramsci, Antonio (1971), *Selections From The Prison Notebooks*, New York: International Publishers.

Greenberg, David and Bystryn, M. (1996), "Capitalism, Bureaucracy and Male Homosexuality," in Steven Seidman ed., *Queer Theory/Sociology*, London: Blackwell Publishers.

Greenberg, Gary and Tobach, Ethel, eds. (1995), *Behavioral Development: Concepts of Approach/Withdrawal and Integrative Levels: The T.C. Schneirla Conference Series*, New York: Garland Publishers.

Gutman, Herbert (1977), *Work, Culture and Society*, New York: Vintage.

Habermas, Jürgen (1981), *Theory of Communicative Action*, New York: Beacon Press.

——(1991), *The Structural Transformation of the Public Sphere*, Cambridge, MA: MIT Press.

Hall, Stuart (1978), "The Hinterland of Science: Ideology and 'the Sociology of Knowledge'," in Bill Schwartz, ed., *On Ideology*, London: Hutchinson.

——(1986), "On Postmodernism and Articulation: An Interview with Stuart Hall," in *Conflicts in Feminism*, M. Hirsh and E. Fox Keller, eds., New York: Routledge, pp. 349–369.

——(1994), *Questions of Cultural Identity*, London and Thousand Oaks, CA: Sage.

Halperin, David (1990), "Homosexuality: A Cultural Construction," an exchange with Richard Schneider, *One Hundred Years of Homosexuality and Other Essays on Greek Love*, New York: Routledge.

——(1995), *Saint Foucault: Toward a Gay Hagiography*, New York: Oxford University Press.

Haraway, Donna (1985), "Situated Knowledge," *Feminist Studies*, 14(3), pp. 575–599.

——(1990), "A Manifesto for Cyborgs: Science, Technology and Socialist Feminism in the 1980s," in Linda J. Nichols, ed., *Feminism / Postmodernism*, New York: Routledge.

Harden, Jacalyn (1997), "Race, Class, Gender and Japanese National Identity," in R.N. Lancaster and M. di Leonardo, eds., *The Gender / Sexuality Reader*, New York: Routledge.

Harris, Daniel (1997), *The Rise and Fall of Gay Culture*, New York: Hyperion.

Harris, Marvin (1968), *The Rise of Anthropological Theory*, New York: Thomas Cromwell.

Harvey, David (1989), *The Condition of Postmodernity: An Enquiry into the Origins of Cultural Exchange*, Oxford: Blackwell.

Hennessy, Rosemary (1992), *Materialist Feminism and the Politics of Discourse*, New York: Routledge.

——(1994), "Queer Theory: Left Politics," *Rethinking Marxism*, 7(3), pp. 85–111.

Herdt, Gilbert (1993), *Third Sex, Third Gender: Beyond Sexual Dimorphism in Culture and History*, New York: Zone Books.

Hilbert, Jeffrey (1995), "The Politics of Drag," in *Out in Culture*, Corey Creekmur and Alexander Doty, eds., Durham: Duke University Press.

Hogan, Steve and Hudson, Lee (1998), *Completely Queer: Gay and Lesbian Encyclopedia*, New York: Henry Holt

Holloway, R.L. (1969), "Culture: A Human Domain?" *Current Anthropology*, 10(4), pp. 395–412.

Horkheimer, Max and Adorno, Theodor W. (1991), *Dialectic of Enlightenment*, New York: Continuum.

Hunt, Linda (1984), *Politics, Culture and Class in the French Revolution*, Berkeley: University of California Press.

Hunt, Sally (1998), *Butch / Femme: Inside Lesbian Gender*, London: Cassell Academic.

Jacoby, Russell (1994), *Dogmatic Wisdom: How the Culture Wars Divert Education and Distract America*, New York: Doubleday.

——(1999), *The End of Utopia: Politics and Culture in an Age of Apathy*, New York: Basic Books.

Jagose, Annamarie (1998), *Queer Theory: An Introduction*, New York: New York University Press.

Jameson, Fredric (1991), *Postmodernism or the Cultural Logic of Late Capitalism*, London: Verso.

——(1995), "Marx's Published Letter," *New Left Review*, 209, pp. 85–98.

——(1998), *The Cultural Turn: Selected Writings on the Postmodern*, London: Verso.

Jameson, Fredric and Masao Miyoshi, eds. (1998), *The Cultures of Globalization*, Durham: Duke University Press.

Janelli, Roger (1993), *Making Capitalism: The Social and Cultural Construction of a South Korean Conglomerate*, Stanford: Stanford University Press.

Jones, G. and Morgan, N., eds. (1994), *Adding Value*, London: Routledge.

Katz, Jonathan (1976), *Gay American History: Lesbians and Gay Men in the USA*, New York: Thomas Cromwell.

——(1990), "The Invention of Homosexuality," *Socialist Review*, 21, pp. 7–34.

——(1996), *The Invention of Heterosexuality*, New York: Penguin.

Kaufman, Cynthia and Martin Joann (1994), "The Chasm of the Political in Postmodern Theory," *Rethinking Marxism*, (7)4, pp. 48–61.

Kessler, Suzanne and McKenna, Wendy (1978), *Gender: An Ethnomethodological Approach*, New York: Wiley.

Kirsch, Max (1998), *In the Wake of the Giant: Multinational Restructuring and Uneven Development in a New England Community*, Albany: SUNY Press.

Kollontai, Alexandra (1996), "Sexual Relations and Class Struggle," in *Material Queer*, Donald Morton, ed., Boulder: Westview.

Kushner, Tony (1995), *Angels in America*, New York: Consortium Books.

Laclau, Ernesto, and Mouffe, Chantal (1985), *Hegemony and Socialist Strategy: Towards a Radical Democratic Politics*, London: Verso.

Lacquer, Thomas, and Gallagher, Catherine, eds. (1987), *The Making of the Modern Body: Sexuality and Society in the Nineteenth Century*, Berkeley: University of California Press.

La Fontaine, J.S. (1985), "Person and Individual: Some Anthropological Reflections," in M. Carritheus, S. Collins, and S. Lukes, eds., *The Category of the Person: Anthropology, Philosophy, History*, Cambridge: Cambridge University Press.

Lamphere, Louise, Ragone, Helene, and Zavella, Patricia (1977), *Situated Lives: Gender and Culture in Everday Life*, London: Routledge.

Lancaster, Roger N. and di Leonardo, Micaela, eds. (1997), *The Gender/Sexuality Reader: Culture, History, Political Economy*, New York: Routledge.

Leacock, Eleanor (1972), "Introduction" to Friedrich Engels, *The Origin of the Family, Private Property and the State*, New York: International Publishers.

——(1981), *Myths of Male Dominance*, New York: Monthly Review Press.

——(1983), "Interpreting the Origins of Gender Inequality: Conceptual and Historical Problems," *Dialectical Anthropology*, 10.

——(1985), "Individuals and Society in Anthropological Theory," *Dialectical Anthropology*, 10, pp. 69–81.

Leacock, Eleanor, ed. (1971), *The Culture of Poverty: A Critique*, New York: Simon and Schuster.

Leacock, Eleanor and Nash, June (1977), "Ideologies of Sex, Archetypes and Sterotypes," *Annals of the New York Academy of Sciences*, 285.

Lee, Martyn J. (1992), *Consumer Culture Reborn: The Cultural Politics of Consumption*, New York: Routledge.

Lenin, V.I. (1993), *The State and Revolution*, New York: Penguin.

Lévi-Strauss, Claude (1973), *Tristes Tropiques*, London: Cape (first published 1955).

Lewis, Oscar (1963), *The Children of Sanchez*, New York: Vintage.

Lilla, Mark (1998), "The Politics of Jacques Derrida," *New York Review of Books* (June 25), 45(11).

Lutz, Catherine and Collins, J.L. (1993), *Reading National Geographic*, Chicago: University of Chicago Press.

——(1997), "Transformations of Homosexuality-Based Classifications," in R.N. Lancaster and M. di Leonardo, eds., *The Gender/Sexuality Reader*, New York: Routledge.

Lynd, Robert and Lynd, Helen (1937), *Middletown in Transition: A Study in Cultural Conflicts*, New York: Harcourt, Brace, and World.

——([1929] 1956) *Middletown: A Study in Contemporary American Culture*, New York: Harcourt, Brace.

Lyotard, Jean-François (1984), *The Postmodern Condition: A Report on Knowledge*, Foreword by Frederick Jameson, Minneapolis: University of Minnesota Press.

——(1993), *Libidual Economy*, Bloomington: Indiana University Press.

MacFarlane, A. (1987), *The Culture of Capitalism*, New York: Basil Blackwell.

MacPherson, C.B. (1964), *The Political Theory of Possessive Individualism*, Oxford: Oxford University Press.

Malinowski, Bronislaw (1984), *Argonauts of the Western Pacific*, New York: Waveland Press.

Mandel, Ernest (1972), *Late Capitalism*, London: Verso.

Mannheim, Karl (1952), *Essays on the Sociology of Knowledge*, London: Routledge and Kegan Paul.

Mantsios, Gregory, ed. (1998), *A New Labor Movement for a New Century*, New York: Monthly Review.

Marcus, G. (1995), "Ethnography in/of the World System," *Annual Review of Anthropology*, 24, pp. 95–117.

Marotta, Toby (1981), *The Politics of Homosexuality*, New York: Houghton Mifflin.

Marx, Karl (1939), *Selected Works*, vol. 1, New York: International Publishers.

——(1967), *Writings of the Young Marx on Philosophy and Society*, ed. and trans. Lloyd D. Easton and Kurt H. Guddat, New York: Doubleday/Anchor Books.

——(1971), *Marx's Grundrisse*, ed. and trans. by David McLellan, London: Macmillan.

——(1973), *The Grundrisse*, New York: Penguin.

——(1976), *Capital*, New York: Penguin.

——(1978), *Grundrisse*, in *The Marx–Engels Reader*, ed. R.C. Tucker, New York: W.W. Norton and Co.

Marx, Karl, and Engels, Friedrich (1939), *The German Ideology*, New York: International Publishers.

——(1959), *Marx and Engels: Basic Writings on Politics and Philosophy*, ed. Lewis Feuer, New York: Anchor Press.

Mazar, Jay (2000), "Labor's New Internationalism," *Foreign Affairs*, 79(2), pp. 81–93.

Mead, Margaret (1935), *Sex and Temperament*, New York: William Morrow.

——(1949), *Male and Female*, New York: William Morrow.

Mellassoux, C. (1972), "From Reproduction to Production," *Economy and Society*, 1(1), pp. 92–105.

Melucci, Alberto (1980), "The New Social Movements," *Social Science Information*, 19, pp. 199–226.

Mészaros, Istvan (1971), "Contingent and Necessary Class Consciousness," in I. Mészaros, ed., *Aspects of History and Class Consciousness*, London: Routledge.

Miller, D. (1996), "Could Shopping Ever Really Matter?" in C. Campbell and P. Falk, eds., *The Shopping Experience*, London: Sage.

——(1997), *Capitalism: An Ethnographic Approach*, Oxford: Berg.

Miller, D., Rowlands, M., and Tilley, C., eds. (1995), *Domination and Resistance*, New York: Routledge.

Mintz, Sidney (1970), "Foreword" to Norman Whitten and John Szwed, eds., *Afro-American Anthropology: Contemporary Perspectives*, New York: Free Press.

——(1985), *Sweetness and Power: The Place of Sugar in Modern History*, New York: Viking.

Money, J. and Ehrhardt, A. (1972), *Man and Woman, Boy and Girl: The Differentiation and Dimorphism of Gender Identity from Conception to Maturity*, Baltimore: Johns Hopkins University Press.

Moody, Kim (1997), *Workers in a Lean World: Unions in the International Economy*, London: Verso.

Morgan, Sandra (1989), *Gender and Anthropology: Critical Reviews of Teaching*, Washington: American Anthropological Association.

Morris, Rosalind C. (1995), "All Made Up: Performance Theory and the New Anthropology of Sex and Gender," *Annual Review of Anthropology*, 24, pp. 567–592.

Morton, Donald, ed. (1996), *The Material Queer: A Lesbigay Cultural Studies Reader*, Boulder: Westview.

Murray, Stephen (1996), *American Gay (Worlds of Desire)*, Chicago: University of Chicago Press.

Nader, Laura (1990), *Harmony Ideology: Justice and Control in a Zapotec Village*, Stanford: Stanford University.

Nanda, Sera (1993), "Hijras: An Alternative Sex and Gender Role," in Gilbert Herdt, ed., *Third Sex, Third Gender: Beyond Sexual Dimorphism in Culture and History*, New York: Zone Books.

Nash, June (1970), *In the Eyes of the Ancestors: Belief and Behavior in a Maya Community*, New Haven: Yale University Press.

——(1977), "Women in Development: Dependency and Exploitation," in *Power, Paradigms and Community Research*, R.J. Liebert and A.W. Imershein, eds., New York: Sage.

——(1978), "The Aztecs and the Ideology of Male Dominance," *Signs*, 4(2), pp. 349–362.

——(1979), *We Eat the Mines and the Mines Eat Us: Dependency and Exploitation in Bolivian Tin Mines*, New York: Columbia University Press.

——(1981), "Ethnographic Aspects of the World Capitalist System," in *Annual Review of Anthropology*, 10, pp. 393–423.

——(1997), "When Isms Become Wasms: Structural Functionalism, Marxism, Feminism and Postmodernism," *Critique of Anthropology*, 17(1), pp. 11–32.

——(forthcoming), *Mayas in the New World Disorder*, New York: Routledge.

Nash, June and Kirsch, Max (1988), "The Discourse of Medical Science in the Construction of Consensus Between Corporation and Community," *Medical Anthropological Quarterly*, Spring, pp. 159–173.

Nash, June and Fernández-Kelley, Patricia (1983), *Women, Men and the International Division of Labor*, Albany: SUNY Press.

Nash, June and Safa, Helen, eds. (1980), *Sex and Class in Latin America*, South Hadley, MA: Bergin and Garvey Publishers.

——(1986), *Women and Change in Latin America*, South Hadley, MA: Bergin and Garvey Publishers.

Newton, Esther (1993), *Cherry Grove, Fire Island: Sixty Years in America's First Gay and Lesbian Town*, Boston: Beacon Press.

Nordquist, Joan (1997), *Queer Theory: A Bibliography*, Santa Cruz: Reference and Research Services.

Norris, W. (1991), "Liberal Attitudes and Homophobic Acts: The Paradoxes of Homosexual Experience in a Liberal Institution," *Journal of Homosexuality*, 22(3/4), pp. 81–220.

O'Laughlin, Bridget (1975), "Marxist Approaches to Anthropology," *Annual Review of Anthropology*, Stanford: Stanford University Press.

Oliver, Kelley (1999), "Agency and Identity: The Future of Feminism," *Studies in Practical Philosophy*, 1(2), pp. 144–166.

——(2000), *Beyond Recognition: Witnessing Subjectivity*, Minneapolis: University of Minnesota Press.

Ollman, Bertell (1971), *Alienation, Marx's Conception of Man in Capitalist Society*, Cambridge: Cambridge University Press.

Ortner, Sherri (1978), *Sherpas Through Their Rituals*, Cambridge: Cambridge University Press.

Pearce, F. and Roberts, A. (1976), "The Social Regulation of Sexual Behavior and Development of Industrial Capitalism in Britain," in Roy Bailey and Jack Youngs, eds., *Contemporary Social Problems in Britain*, Lexington, MA: Lexington Books.

Phelan, Shane (1989), *Identity Politics: Lesbian Feminism and the Limits of Community*, Philadelphia: Temple University Press.

——(1993), "(Be)Coming Out: Lesbian Identity and Politics," *Signs*, 18(4), pp. 765–790.

Piettrykowski, Bruce (1994), "Consuming Culture: Postmodernism, Post-Fordism and Economics," *Rethinking Marxism*, 7(1).

Plummer, Ken (1992), *Modern Homosexualities: Fragments of Lesbian and Gay Experience*, London: Routledge.

Polanyi, Karl, Arensberg, Conrad, M., and Pearson, Harry W. (1957), *Trade and Market in the Early Empires: Economies in History and Theory*, New York: The Free Press.

Poster, Mark (1989), *Critical Theory and Poststructuralism*, Ithaca: Cornell University Press.

Rabinow, Paul, ed. (1984), *The Foucault Reader*, New York: Pantheon.

Raffo, Susan (1997), *Queerly Classed*, Boston: South End Press.

Reiter, Rayna R., ed. (1975), *Toward an Anthropology of Women*, New York: Monthly Review Press.

Rhrlich-Levitt, Ruby, Sykes, Barbara and Weatherford, Elizabeth (1975), "Aboriginal Women: Male and Female Anthropology Perspectives," in Rayna R. Reiter, ed., *Toward an Anthropology of Women*, New York: Monthly Review Press.

Rorty, Richard (1979), *Philosophy and the Mirror of the Nature*, New Jersey: Princeton University Press.

——(1991), *Objectivity, Relativism and Trust*, Cambridge: Cambridge University Press.

Rosenau, Pauline Marie (1992), *Postmodernism and the Social Sciences*, Princeton, NJ: Princeton University Press.

Ross, Ellen and Rapp, Rayna (1997), "Sex and Society: A Research Note from Social History and Anthropology," in R.N. Lancaster and M. di Leonardo, eds., *The Gender/Sexuality Reader*, New York: Routledge.

Rostow, Walter Whitman (1960), *The Stages of Economic Growth: A Non-Communist Manifesto*, Cambridge: Cambridge University Press.

Rowlands, Mark (1995), "The Material Culture of Success," in J. Friedman, ed., *Consumption and Identity*, London: Howard, pp.147–166.

Sacks, Karen (1975), "Engels Revisited: Women, The Organization of Production, and Private Property," in Rayna R. Reiter, ed., *Toward an Anthropology of Women*, New York: Monthly Review Press.

Safa, Helen (1981), "Runaway Shops and Female Employment: the Search for Cheap Labor," In *Signs*, 7(2), pp. 418–433.

——(1983), "Women, Production and Reproduction in Industrial Capitalism: A Comparison of US and Brazil Factory Workers," in June Nash and Patricia Fernández-Kelly, eds., *Women, Men, and the International Division of Labor*, Albany: SUNY Press.

Sahlins, Marshall D. and Service, Elman R. (1970), *Evolution and Culture*, Ann Arbor: The University of Michigan Press.

Said, Edward (1993), *Culture and Imperialism*, New York: Knopf.

Salokar, Rebecca Mae (1998), "Begin Gay Rights Litigation: Using a Systematic Strategy to Effect Political Change in the United States," *Gay and Lesbian Quarterly*, 3, pp. 385–416.

Sapir, David, and Crocker, J. Christopher, eds. (1944), *The Social Uses of Metaphor: Essays on the Anthropology of Rhetoric*, Philadelphia: University of Pennsylvania Press.

Schneider, David (1968), *American Kinship*, New Jersey: Prentice Hall.

Schneider, Richard, Jr., ed. (1998), *The Best of Harvard Gay and Lesbian Review*, Philadelphia: Temple University Press.

Schor, Naomi, and Weed, Elizabeth, eds. (1998), *Feminism Meets Queer Theory*, Bloomington: Indiana University Press.

Scott, Joan (1988), *Gender and the Politics of History*, New York: Columbia University Press.

——(1993), "The Evidence of Experience," in H. Abelove, M.A. Barale, and D. Halperin, eds., *The Lesbian and Gay Studies Reader*, London: Routledge, pp. 397–415.

Sedgwick, Eve Kosofsky (1985), *Between Men: English Literature and Male Homosexual Desire*, New York: Columbia University Press.

——(1990), *Epistemology of the Closet*, Berkeley: University of California Press.

Seidman, Gay W. (1994), *Manufacturing Militance*, Berkeley: University of California Press.

Seidman, Steven (1997), *Difference Troubles*, Cambridge: Cambridge University Press.

Seidman, Steven, ed. (1996), *Queer Theory / Sociology*, Oxford: Blackwell Publishers.

Séve, Lucien (1978), *Man in Marxist Theory and the Psychological of the Personality*, trans. John McGreen, New Jersey: Humanities Press.

Shostak, Margorie (1981), *Nisa: The Life and Words of a !Kung Woman*, Cambridge, MA: Harvard University Press.

Siegel, Lee (1998), "The Gay Science," *The New Republic*, November 9, pp. 30–42.

Signorile, Michelangelo (1993), *Queer in America: Sex, the Media, and the Closets of Power*, New York: Random House.

——(1997), *Life on the Outside: The Signorile Report on Gay Men, Sex, Drugs, Muscles, and the Passages of Life*, New York: HarperCollins Publishers.

Silverblatt, Irene (1987), *Moon, Sun and Witches: Gender Ideologies and Class in Inca and Colonial Perú*, New Jersey: Princeton University Press.

Simpson, Mark (1996), *Anti-Gay: Homosexuality and Its Discontents*, London: Cassell.

Siskind, J. (1978), "Kinship Relations of Production," *American Anthropologist*, 80.

Sklair, Leslie (1991), *Sociology of the Global System*, Baltimore: John Hopkins University Press.

——(1998), "Social Movements and Global Capitalism," in Fredric Jameson and Masao Miyoshi, eds., *The Cultures of Globalization*, Durham: Duke University Press.

Smith, Steven (1992), *Gender Thinking*, Philadelphia: Temple University Press.

Snitow, Ann, Stansell, Christine, and Thompson, Sharon, eds. (1983), *Powers of Desire: The Politics of Sexuality*, New York: Monthly Review.

Sommerville, Siobhan (1997), "Scientific Racism and the Invention of the Homosexual Body," in R.N. Lancaster and M. di Leonardo, eds., *The Gender / Sexuality Reader*, New York: Routledge.

Spivak, Gayatri Chakravorty (1987), *In Other Worlds*, New York: Methuen.

Stabile, Carole A. (1994), "Feminism without Guarantees: The Misalliances and Missed Alliances of Postmodern Social Theory," *Rethinking Marxism*, 7(1), pp. 48–61.

Stein, Edward (1992), *Forms of Desire: Sexual Orientation and the Social Constructionist Controversy*, New York: Routledge.

Stockton, Kathryn (1996), "What can Materialism Mean to Poststructuralists," in David Morton, ed., *Material Queer*, Boulder: Westview.

Stoler, Ann (1977), "Making Empire Respectable: The Politics of Race and Sexual Morality in Twentieth Century Colonial Cultures," in L. Lamphere, H. Ragone, and P. Zavella, eds., *Situated Lives: Gender and Culture in Everyday Life*, London: Routledge.

Strathern, Marilyn (1995), *The Relation: Issues in Complexity and Scale*, Cambridge: Prickly Pear Press.

Swan, Wallace, ed. (1997), *Gay, Lesbian / Bisexual / Transgender Public Policy Issues: A Citizen's and Administration's Guide to the New Cultural Struggle*, New York: Harrington Park Press.

Talal Asad, ed. (1973), *Anthropology and the Colonial Encounter*, New York: Humanities Press.

Therborn, Göran (1980), *The Ideology of Power and the Power of Ideology*, London: Blackwell.

Thompson. E.P. (1980), *The Making of the English Working Class*, London: Victor Gollancz.

Thompson, John B. (1990), *Ideology and Modern Culture*, Stanford: Stanford University Press.

Timpanaro, Sebastiano (1970), *On Materialism*, London: New Left Books.

Tomlinson, John (1999), *Globalization and Culture*, Chicago: University of Chicago Press.

Touraine, Alain (1981), *The Voice and the Eye*, Cambridge: Cambridge University Press.

Trotsky, Leon (1973), *Problems of Everyday Life*, New York: Pathfinder Press.

Trumbach, Randolph (1993), "London's Sapphists: From Three Sexes to Four Genders in the Making of Modern Culture," in Gilbert Herdt, ed., *Third Sex, Third Gender: Beyond Sexual Dimorphism in Culture and History*, New York: Zone Books.

Vaid, Urvashi (1995), *Virtual Equality: The Mainstreaming of Lesbian and Gay Liberation*, New York: Anchor.

Valocchi, Steve (n.d.), "The Old Left, the New Left, and Gay Liberation: Coming Together, Falling Apart," unpublished manuscript.

Vance, Carol (1984), *Pleasure and Danger*, London: Routledge and Keegan Paul.

Venable, Vernon (1946), *Human Nature: The Marxian View*, London: Dennis Dobson.

Vlahos, O. (1979), *Body: The Ultimate Symbol*, New York: Lippen Cott.

Walters, Suzanna (1996), "From Here to Queer: Radical Feminism, Postmodernism, and the Lesbian Menace (or Why can't a Woman be more Like a Fag?)," *Signs*, 21(4).

Warner, Michael (1993), *Fear of a Queer Planet*, Minneapolis: University of Minnesota Press.

Warren, Kay B. (1999), *Indigenous Movements and Their Critics: Pan Mayan Activism in Guatemala*, Princeton: Princeton University Press.

Weber, Alexander (1990), "Lyotard's Combative Theory of Discourse," *Telos* 83, pp. 141–150.

Weeks, Jeffrey (1985), *Sexuality and Its Discontents*, London: Routledge and Kegan Paul.

——(1993), "Capitalism and Gay Identity," in H. Abalove, M.A. Barale, and D. Halperin, eds., *The Lesbian and Gay Studies Reader*, New York and London: Routledge.

——(1995), *Invented Moralities: Sexual Values in an Age of Uncertainty*, New York: Columbia University Press.

Weeks, Jeffrey and Holland, Jaret, eds. (1996), *Sexual Cultures, Communities, Values and Intimacy*, New York: St Martin's Press.

Whiley, Susan (1977), "Women and Hindu Tradition," *Signs*, 3.

White, Edmund (1997), "The Personal is Political," in M. Duberman, ed. *Queer Representations: Reading Lives, Reading Cultures: A Center for Lesbian and Gay Studies Book*, New York: New York University Press.

White, Leslie A. (1949), *The Science of Culture*, New York: Farrar, Straus and Giroux.

Williams, Gwynn A. (1960), "Gramsci's Concept of Hegemony," *Journal of the History of Ideas*, 21, pp. 586–599.

Williams, Patricia (1991), *The Alchemy of Race and Rights*, Cambridge: Harvard University Press.

Williams, Raymond (1958), "Culture is Ordinary," reprinted in his *Resources of Hope* (1988), London: Verso.

——(1985), *Culture and Society: 1780–1950*, London: Harmondsworth.

Willis, Susan (1993), "Disney World, Public Use, Private State," *The South Atlantic Quarterly*, Winter, 92(1).

Wolf, Eric R. (1957), "Close Corporate Communities in Mesoamerica and Central Java," *Southwestern Journal of Anthropology*, 13, pp. 1–18.

——(1959), "Specific Aspects of Plantation Systems in the New World: Community Subcultures and Social Class," in *Plantation Systems of the New World: Papers and Discussion Summaries of the Seminar Held in San Juan, Puerto Rico*, Washington DC: Pan American Union.

——(1982), *Europe and the People Without History*, Berkeley: University of California Press.

——(1999), *Envisioning Power: Ideologies of Dominance and Crisis*, Berkeley: University of California Press.

Wolfe, Susan J. and Penelope, Julia (1993), "Sexual Identity/Textual Politics," *http://www.lesbian.org/amy/essay/bf-paper.html*

Wolfson, Charles (1982), *The Labor Theory of Culture*, London: Routledge.

Wood, Ellen Meiksins (1986), *The Retreat from Class: A New "True" Socialism*, London: Verso.

Wright, Eric Olin (1993), "Class Analysis, History of Emancipation," *New Left Review*, 202.

Yingling, Thomas (1991), "AIDS in America: Postmodern Governance, Identity of experience," in Diana Fuss, ed., *Inside/Out*, New York: Routledge.

Zhang, Xudong (1999), "Postmodernism and Post-Socialist Society: Cultural Politics in China After the 'New Era'," *New Left Review*, 237, pp. 77–105.

# Index

master narratives 72
Mattachine Society 107–8
Mauss, Marcel 43
Mayans 120
Mead, Margaret 49
medicalization 67
Mészaros, Istvan 81
meta-identity 1, 2, 86
meta-narrative 3, 124
Miller, D. 70
modernism 19
modernization theory 55–7
Moody, Kim 39, 119
Morris, Rosalind 87
Moufe, Chantal 85
Multilateral Agreement on Investment
    (MAI) 98
multinational corporations 77, 98, 108–9,
    118; and community 68–9; and energy
    104; and strategies of resistance 120

Nader, Laura 82
Nanda, Sera 52
Nash, June 50, 62, 70, 77, 113, 120
National Organization of Women 109
nature: and gender 50
new social movements 80–1, 119
newness 75
Newton, Ester 136
Nicholson, Linda 102
Nietzsche, Friedrich 20
normativity 36
North American Free Trade Agreement
    (NAFTA) 98

observation 2
O'Laughlin, Bridget 5, 102
Ollman, Bertell 132
Ortner, Sherri 49

parody 89, 90, 91, 92, 93
part-cultures 115–117
particularism 5
Pearce, F. 50, 66, 68
Penelope, Julia 7, 81

performance 86, 87, 90
performativity 18, 86–90
political 97, 98–100
political economy 5
politics 16, 98, 102, 110; and lifestyle 72–3
post-structuralism 8–9, 35, 84–5, 114;
    language 42; and postmodernism 28–
    30; and Queer theory 33
Poster, Mark 27
postmodernism 4, 84–5, 114; discourse
    24–8; Foucault 21–4; individual 116;
    and post-structuralism 28–30; and
    postmodernity 19–20; and Queer
    theory 33–4
postmodernity 28; and postmodernism
    19–20
power 9, 16, 36, 80, 111; Butler 86;
    Foucault 21–2, 23, 24; and gender 50;
    and ideology 40–2; Queer theory 42–3
production 26, 57, 66–7
project identity 6, 101

quasi-identity 1, 2
queer communities 115–16; as part-
    cultures 116–17
queer culture 74
queer identities: and capitalism 66–7
Queer Nation 33, 109
Queer theory 2–3, 17–19, 32, 121–3;
    academic context 30–31; beginnings
    32–4; class 38–40; consequences 114–
    15; culture 43–5; and diversity 35–7;
    interdeterminacy 34–5; paradox 42–3

Rabinow, Paul 24
Raffo, Susan 39, 40, 128
Ragone, Helena 44
Rapp, Rayna 53
rationality 19–20
reality 61
Reagan, Ronald 17
Reiter, Rayna R. 49
resistance 82, 86, 121; strategies 117–18,
    120–1; and identity 6–7
resistance identity 6–7, 32